Marriage and Divorce Hardships

Enhanced Edition

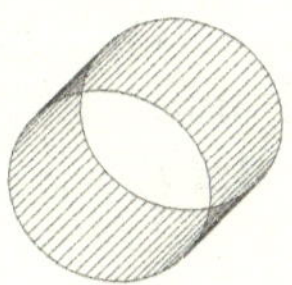

Author's Books

(As of June 20, 2020)*

Non-fiction

The Nature of Love and Relationships 2011, **2016**
Doubts and Decisions for Living:
Volume I: The Foundation of Human Thoughts **2014**
Volume II: The Sanctity of Human Spirit **2014**
Volume III: The Structure of Human Life **2014**
Relationship Facts, Trends, and Choices **2016**
The Mysteries of Life, Love, and Happiness **2016**
Marriage and Divorce Hardships **2016**
Gender Qualities, Quirks, and Quarrels **2016**
Relationship Needs, Framework, and Models **2016**
Being Better Beings **2020**

Fiction

Persian Moons 2007, **2016**
Midnight Gate-opener 2011, **2016**
My Lousy Life Stories **2014**
Persian Suns **2021 (Planned)**

---

*12 older books are Enhanced Editions and printed in 2020. They were resubmitted to the Library and Archives Canada Cataloguing as well. If a book's 'print date' on the copyright page is older, the newest version is available at Amazon and bookstores.

Love and Relationships Series
3

Marriage and Divorce Hardships

(Inevitable Traps)

Tom Omidi, Ph.D.

Love and Relationships Series # 3

Omidi, Tom, 1945-
Marriage and divorce hardships : inevitable traps
/ Tom Omidi.

(Love and relationships series ; 3)
ISBN 978-1-988351-06-3 (paperback)

1. Marriage--Psychological aspects. 2. Man-woman relationships. 3. Interpersonal relations. I. Title.

Old edition at
Library and Archives Canada Cataloguing in Publication
HQ801.O445 2016 306.8 C2016-902406-7

Published by Eros Books,
Vancouver, British Columbia
Canada

erosbooks2020.@gmail.com

Enhanced and Printed in 2020

Contents

Contents (Cont.)

List of Tables

INTRODUCTION

While humans can never elude life's hardships, causing so much of them ourselves, especially in our relationships, shows the collapse of our personalities and cultures. It reveals many sad facts about humans' debility to think straight and relate to each other peacefully. It shows our neglect for letting societies get so hectic in our allegedly modern civilization. It reflects that, after so many millenniums of trials and errors, we have failed horribly to design a viable means of coexisting without hurting one another so much regularly. Then, we wonder why we are all so lost like this? Is it because humans are inherently incapable of relating, especially in their marriages? Or, is it just because we are not intelligent enough to figure out, or agree about, relationships' needs and objectives? Or, are we simply too mulish and selfish to relate in any relationship, despite our obsession to have a soul mate or at least a reliable companion? Nonetheless, our oblivion about the rising social folly due to human arrogance and ignorance is just amazing!

Ironically, our lousy relationships raise our lives' hardships and in return life's growing pressures make our marriages less bearable and manageable. Thus, it seems that the only way out of this vicious cycle is to develop better means of relating in families in order to alleviate personal and social pains around the globe largely.

Discussing humans' big role in personal and social agonies, while raising life's dilemmas and hardships too, requires many volumes. The goal here is to focus on personal hardships and naïveté related to our marital relationships. Yet, this study also reveals how a good bulk of prevalent personal shortfalls leads to societal stress and alienation. To start, we can ask ourselves the following basic questions.

1. Do we know the realistic **marriage purposes**?
2. Do we recognize the depth of **relationship challenges**?
3. What could be the **outcome of our oblivion** about marital mayhems causing us so much personal hardships, not to mention all the ensuing chaos in society?

Marriage Purposes

The answer to the first question is a resounding ‘NO.’ We have lost track of our senses about this basic human need. We have lost our instincts about the purposes of marriage over the years and even eradicated that basic knowledge of ‘marriage objectives’ that religions and old cultures had injected in our heads. Now, we are so horribly untrained and uncertain about marriage objectives. At the same time, we are still adamant to fulfil too many of our personal needs through our relationships according to our naïve and crooked views of individualism, equality, and happiness.

People marry due to physical attraction, lust, biological clock, social/family pressure, love deficiency, psychological needs, happiness illusion, loneliness, misperceptions, financial issues, obsessions, insecurity, or just for no particular reason. If we ponder our own reasons for marrying, or ask others about theirs, the answers are usually absurd and surprising. They show the depth of our vastly low knowledge of marriage objectives and our shoddy criteria for choosing a companion. As an example, in a group therapy session, divorced subjects were asked about their reasons for marrying their ex-spouses.

The typical answers were quite informative, as noted below:

- I loved him/her (the most popular answer)
- Mother/father figure
- Out of pity, I felt sorry for her/him
- Lifestyle change
- To have a family (mostly children)
- To stabilize my life or to have a home

While all these views might have some personal merits, they do not offer a comprehensive, consistent perception about realistic marriage purposes. In fact, they have nothing to do with the sensible purposes of marriage in line with the ones reviewed in Chapter One. Accordingly, people's understanding of 'success factors' in relationships are also shallow and futile. At best, people list longevity, communication, security, love, wealth, etc. as valid criteria for success. Those with negative experiences in relationships are cynical about the possibility of ever building peaceful marriages, anyway. To them, modern relationships can be nothing but hell.

Nowadays, we have created our own crude, subjective ideas about the purposes and potentials of relationships according to our personal needs and superficial values around us. We live in fantasy regarding relationships' nature and particular needs. Therefore, we set ourselves up for failure, because our naïve expectations cannot be fulfilled. We (as a society) no longer have a common grasp of relationships and their purposes, let alone the knowledge of the factors making them successful. Our educational systems, especially at senior high school, have failed to teach this essential subject to the youths who need this primary wisdom so urgently. It is a pity that such a crucial matter, with such grave effect on social wellbeing, is left to people's personal interpretations, instead of being researched and propagated for everybody's benefit.

Now, nobody really knows the parameters and objectives of a successful relationship due to rapid social changes that have tainted most people's personalities and perceptions about relationships. Thus, when the initial purpose of a relationship is not valid or solid, the chances of keeping it functional would be quite slim. After a while, couples realize their mistakes and begin to resent their partners and themselves for being dragged into a relationship incapable of satisfying their varied needs, which are superficial and whimsical most often, anyway.

In all, to resolve the existing chaos, the whole society must show willingness and patience to gauge relationships' special needs in our progressive societies. We should challenge our present mentality about relationships by studying the viability of people's rising personal needs and expectations from their relationships in the new era. In fact, 'relationships' must now be viewed as a unique entity with its own specific needs. For sure, the process of understanding these needs and developing some principles for relationships would be gradual, because couples must initially learn to reduce their expectations from relationships, and instead attend to their personal needs more independently. That would be a tough job but rather urgent.

Accordingly, this book intends to address our negligence in causing the rising personal and social instability, too. It offers means of revamping our mentalities and relating effectively in our marriages—or at least eluding this potential source of pain by learning to live somewhat more independently. Instead of just bragging about independence, time has come to become self-reliant truly, which ironically teaches us the art of relating and relying on one another in a realistic manner as well.

Life's torments and traps are inevitable facts. Yet, they are now growing too fast due to our weird expectations from life and relationships. Family conflicts are singeing our spirits and endless dilemmas are besieging our brains. Only the type and depth of our hardships vary in line with our personal resilience and intelligence to handle them patiently. We try to foresee and face life hurdles boldly, but our low grasp of marriage and divorce variables and consequences remain a big hurdle.

Relationship Challenges

The answer to the second question (on Page 2) is a resounding 'NO' as well. People have no grasp of relationships' needs and challenges due to the ambiguity of social structure, culture, values, and couples' high expectations from relationships and life. Couples have no idea what they are getting into and how to prepare themselves for those challenges proactively. They try to cope with a large variety of pressures and problems without addressing the sources of the growing chaos in society and relationships. In fact, our modern society appears too lax or ignorant about the roots of pandemic marriage conundrums. We do not seem serious about facing this sad reality and admit to the necessity of fundamental changes and vast efforts. For one thing, we have not developed progressive mentalities and relationship models in line with people's modern lifestyles and needs. Ultimately, the question is whether we can still hope to bring some objectivity back into relationships, or do we wish to merely dream and live so helplessly within the accelerating relationship chaos? Can we ever realize how our rampant life priorities and misperceptions along with our naïve demands from relationships are causing us so much added hardships?

Naturally, modern social values goading individualism and pomposity are responsible for people's lack of objectivity about relationships and crooked mentalities altogether. In return, our demented mentalities and approaches are damaging the social structure and values too fast. This vicious cycle is getting out of control, to what disastrous end, only God might know! All along, we face complex dilemmas and sad questions, such as: Are we just victims of low social morality, poor conscience, and a lack of direction? Are we now fully lost and hypnotized to the point of causing ourselves so much suffering without a sense to stop and ponder the effects of our infected mentalities and the likely outcome of our present oblivion for the whole humanity?

Outcome of Our Oblivion *(3rd question raised above, Page 2)*

The effects of relationship hardships on people and society are rather obvious to most of us. The repercussions of our naïve mentalities and assumptions about relationships' potentials and purposes are overwhelming us, too, as we merely follow the crowd within such a vile, confusing setting. It feels bizarre that we do this to ourselves so recklessly! Our reluctance to see or acknowledge the depth of the relationship dilemmas we have imposed upon ourselves, as well as their personal and social ramifications, is quite shocking. In fact, our ignorance, apathy, or denial shows the depth of our social numbness. Simply, our oblivion about the causes of all these pains feels baffling.

Discussions in the future chapters will reveal the severity of relationship conundrums and challenges in the new era in line with the depth of our misperceptions about relationships. For one thing, our mirage of marriage as a romantic and happy experience has confused us so universally. We have no sense regarding the agonies that it often adds to our already stressful lives, especially in relation to what we expect to accomplish in a marriage. Then, on top of its unique hardships, marriage also forces us into the complex hassles of separation, divorce, and single parenthood. Recognizing these facts might encourage us reflect and seek solutions for this big social pandemic more actively. **By the way, the word 'relationships' in this book mainly implies 'marital relationships' whether couples are formally married or not.**

Overall, so many relationship challenges are overwhelming us, in particular the new generations, as reviewed in this book along with an analysis of marriage purposes. Now, suddenly, bearing marriage and divorce hardships are inevitable facts we have imposed upon ourselves due to our naïveté and arrogance. Yet, the ultimate questions we can ask ourselves are, 'Whether viable solutions exist for our rising folly and if humans might ever mature enough to find them.'

PART I

Marriage

A Cautionary Note

This book's approach to the delicate matter of marriage feels rather academic and formal in some parts, besides demanding lots of efforts and thinking to grasp and manage our marital needs and complications. The author realizes readily that most of us lack the patience, time, and incentive to study and apply this book's suggestions. The customary ways of handling our marriages, especially its romantic aspects, feels adequate and more natural to us as well without the need to get too rigid and scientific about it.

Still, the rise of relationship hurdles and deficiencies in the new era and the immense damages our marriage and divorce decisions are inflicting on people's psyches and society overall is now getting out of hand. Accordingly, the author believes that changing people's attitude about marriage and divorce is a serious social matter that needs immediate attention somehow!

This and a handful other books about relationships by this author had to identify most relevant factors needing scrutiny in a rather complete and academic presentation. However, these points can be reproduced gradually in smaller pamphlets for addressing each topic more directly and a bit less formally.

Anyway, reading these unorthodox ideas slowly and trying to digest the details with patience can save us lots of time and hassle in our marriages and lead to a happier life. Looking for quick fixes or speed reading the material would be futile.

In fact, governments and scholars must attend to this matter and teach these basics at high schools to prepare people for the hassles and joys of marriage if we just learn how to handle this sensitive matter wisely in our irresponsible modern societies.

CHAPTER ONE
Relationship Purposes

The *ultimate objective* of relationships (marriage) is to help couples face life's hardships together and reduce each other's burdens. The ten plausible relationship purposes listed below are based on the author's studies and discussions in his other books about love and relationships. Mainly, couples' prevalent expectations from marriage were grouped into two: A) Sensible Expectations (marriage purposes) that seem viable in modern lifestyles and, B) Irrelevant (Ideal) Expectations (marriage purposes) that are simply incompatible with people's zeal for happiness, individualism, equality, and pleasure in our modern world. This chapter studies these expectations. Some other related analyses of marital parameters are included in this author's book, *Relationship Needs, Framework, and Models.*

A. Sensible Relationship Purposes

The following ten sensible relationship purposes are relevant and useful for running a healthy marriage in the new era, while partners value their independence and personal careers.

1. Sex
2. Communication
3. Compassion
4. Companionship
5. Teamwork
6. MLove (tactful, adaptation love)
7. Friendship
8. Respect-Social acceptance
9. Personal Success
10. Financial Stability

Relationships might bring love and happiness to couples, too, but not as their main objectives. The lack of adequate love or happiness is often due to our personal deficiencies on the top of our exaggerated expectations from life and relationships. The reason for so many relationship failures, nowadays, is that our present mentalities are unaligned with reality. We have no grasp of relationship purposes, especially its ultimate objective of making life just a bit more bearable for partners. That is all! Strangely, most of us have never appreciated the real purposes of relationships and the high degree of patience and flexibility required. Instead, we trust our imaginations and Egos to define some arbitrary notions. Thus, we often fail.

With these main needs and objectives of relationships in mind, let us review its other sensible purposes.

1. Sex: This is the most logical expectation from relationships. Since couples *attempt* not to look outside their relationships to fulfil this urge, they should depend on their partners to satisfy this essential need. In fact, sex could be considered a primary purpose (or outcome) of relationships, since partners' basic need for sex becomes ethically restricted based on the big assumption that relationships could and would satisfy this need. In reality, however, partners often withdraw sex as a tool for emotional blackmail or retaliation. Besides, sometimes partners cannot cooperate in this regard, thus look for sex elsewhere. Anyway, this is a valid objective for relationships. The large variety of dramas surrounding sex cannot be helped, either. Most of them are psychologically explainable and rather inevitable. The only advice is to grasp the role of sex realistically, instead of using it recklessly for blackmailing and hurting our partners.

2. Communication: Effective communication is certainly the essence of successful relationships, especially for enforcing teamwork. Thus, it is a big purpose for relationships. Yet, many fine relationships are ruined, nowadays, due to misperceptions and miscommunications. Partners' oversensitivity, arrogance, and false pride usually obstruct even their common dialogues.

Effective communication is also important for implementing a hassle-free process of separation when necessary. Instead of spending time and money on lawyers, a prenuptial contract, as well as partners' objectivity, could boost communication when separation seems inevitable. Anyway, effective communication is the toughest objective of relationships, because most often partners are not properly trained for it, or because retaliation and Ego make their communication too difficult to manage.

3. **Compassion:** Exchanging compassion is a logical purpose of relationships. However, it seldom materializes at the desired level, because everybody seeks more compassion every day, while the number of humble and patient people in society is shrinking. Thus, it is wise to set our expectations rather low for receiving true compassion in relationships, nowadays.

The problem is that we always crave sympathy, but have difficulty expressing it ourselves. Often we feel our partners' needs are too superfluous and selfish. It is demanded too often or the nature of their expectations seems unreasonable to us. Therefore, the supply and demand for compassion are vastly unbalanced in societies and across the nations, due to people's growing oversensitivity and neediness, on top of the rising life hardships. Yet, instead of grasping this general shortfall of human nature, we take the matter personally and turn against our partners when they cannot give us as much compassion as we seek. We do not notice our own inability to offer genuine sympathy often enough, but we are needy for it so relentlessly.

On the one hand, couples should realize that expecting true sympathy is unrealistic in a modern society where the supply and demand for compassion are unbalanced—mostly due to innate human nature. Stress and depression have simply made us vulnerable and too needy for sympathy, but there is nobody out there to give it to us.

On the other hand, compassion is a sensible objective for relationships—with a major reservation about its nature and source, and since fulfilling it is not easy. Thus, a more realistic definition for compassion, nowadays, should stress mostly on our personal ability to induce it, instead of craving it. The best way to achieve this goal is to become a better person and show more compassion to others, instead of demanding it. *At best,* we might expect compassion only if we are good at generating it ourselves. Merely needing something does not entitle us for it. The irony is that the more we learn to give compassion, the higher our chance for receiving it becomes, and the less we feel the need for phony sympathies, anyway. By learning to become a compassionate individual, we become self-sufficient largely and possibly get a lot in return, too. Thus, in a sense, we can generate the compassion that we need personally. Only this type of mindset can curb our depression and dependence on people and psychiatrists to manage our lives. The need for compassion is too strong and urgent these days to ignore, after all. Especially, the need to grow patience and flexibility must be taken as inherent means and mission of compassion.

Another crucial point is that, while compassion is an ideal personal attribute, knowing how to appreciate, acknowledge, and learn from people's compassion towards us is even more urgent and important. We must know how to not only receive and return compassion, but also manage our lives personally, so that we are not too needy for compassion and other people's assistance (or approval) as a way of living.

4. Companionship: This is a given outcome of relationships, but we do not quite know its purpose or the ways of benefiting from this basic privilege of relationships. We all like to have a partner, and relationships provide this chance, but the question is if we prefer a lousy companion to loneliness. Conversely, finding an ideal partner is a matter of luck and often a doomed expectation, too. We all seek high-quality companions to get love and compassion. A companion must be like this or that, we imagine, while we strive to satisfy our urge for love.

In all, we have no proper education about the purpose and process of companionship. Thus, our initial perceptions about marriage and our companion usually prove to be erroneous before long. In fact, we alienate our partners fast based on our past and present misperceptions, besides our inherent egoism.

The comments made before about the supply and demand for compassion and love, apply to companionship, too.

5. Teamwork: An important purpose of relationships is to create synergy through teamwork. In addition, as we insist on more independence and individualism, the need for teamwork becomes greater in order to keep our Egos under a leash. For teamwork, partners must surely have some genuine qualities, including modesty and objectivity. However, we face more *obsessions for individualism,* nowadays, instead of *modesty.* Therefore, finding partners of such quality and implementing teamwork in relationships would be a big challenge. Anyway, teamwork is an absolute purpose of relationships.

6. MLove: As explained in the next section (under Irrelevant Relationship Purposes) love is not a purpose of relationships in general. Instead, partners need some civilized and genuine *love attitude* towards each other in order to relate effectively. This narrow meaning of love (MLove) is a sensible purpose for marriages. It refers to couples' discreet expressions of love to show compassion and social etiquette, and to relate smoothly.

Many radical ideas have been proposed in this book. They might make the nature of our relationships appear too dry and impersonal. Yet, this picture of pessimism might prove to be the reality that we should eventually face based on the values and culture we are embracing so fast, most often inadvertently. Thus, MLove is a helpful and relatively realistic expectation to induce passion in relationships. It reminds partners of the need to keep working on their relationship and communication.

7. Friendship: A good test of ‘relationship success’ would be partners' ability to enhance their friendship. However, this idea has never been promoted as a relationship purpose. Often, couples actually prove their inability to be friends, but still insist naively to build a relationship. Surely, the main feature of successful friendships, which is missing in relationships, is that friends' limited expectations grow gradually and naturally without pressure or demand. Then, even if those expectations are not fulfilled, they seldom argue or fight over them. They only moderate (realign) their own expectations to keep their friendship. They value their friendship so much they willingly reduce their expectations. This is indeed the strength of good friendships and a main reason for their success and longevity. This is exactly an opposite mentality prevalent in relationships, nowadays. Now, spouses set tough expectations immediately, instead of appreciating the value of what they already have, like the way friends do. In fact, couples keep increasing their demands and expectations, and nag all the time, too, until their relationships fall apart. Thus, partners' aptitude for friendship should be promoted as a major purpose for relationships and analysed actively. Marital relationships should be expected to rely more on friendship than love.

8. Respect/Social Acceptance: As part of our struggle for equality, independence, and identity, couples demand respect from their partners, nowadays, in line with social trends. Thus, it is an acceptable purpose for relationships. However, partners must not only expect respect. Rather, they should learn how to respect their partners, despite their obvious idiosyncrasies and personality weaknesses.

Society gives a higher status to family than individuals. We personally value our relationships highly for many reasons as well, but mainly for fitting better within the society. This is an automatic by-product and expectation from relationships.

9. Personal Success: A relationship should facilitate partners' personal ambitions and success. Although sounding personal, or even selfish, partners' successes boost their relationships in two ways. First, by stressing on personal success, partners try to find the appropriate relationship model that can best fulfil their essential personal needs, or else they would not even bother getting into a risky relationship. Second, if partners feel happy and fulfilled individually, their relationship's chance of success also grows a lot—and vice versa. It makes total sense.

Partners' cooperation is expected to give them a higher chance for success in social and personal endeavours. Synergy and moral support are the main objectives of companionship. Thus, personal success is a reasonable and helpful criterion to include in the list of sensible relationship purposes. Sadly, in reality, the very sense of individualism and independence forces partners to compete with each other. Their unrelenting urges for recognition and showing off their independence and identity make them too arrogant at the expense of losing their relationship. Therefore, couples must not only choose the right relationship model based on their personalities and need for personal achievements, but also keep their Egos under a leash.

10. Financial Stability: An implied and important purpose of relationships is to force a degree of financial stability for their family's welfare. Partners must have adequate financial sense and cooperate in securing the needed financial resources, but also avoid waste and extravagance in line with a long-term plan for their financial security.

B. Irrelevant (Ideal) Relationship Purposes

Irrelevant relationship purposes reflect our idealistic picture of marriage that cannot materialize normally in modern societies where people seek happiness, love, and independence as their basic rights. Thus, this set of ideals cannot be viewed practical. As partners learn not to fuss about these ideals so much, they can use their energies and brains more effectively on fulfilling the sensible purposes discussed above to make their marriages successful without necessarily satisfying the ones discussed below. These ideals might happen as fringe benefits of a good marriage, but not as a norm. Thus, partners must build proper mindsets to never count on, or demand, them from each other.

1. Dependence
2. Security
3. SLove
4. ELove
5. Trust
6. Happiness
7. Commitment
8. Longevity

1. Dependence: Partners' attempts to align their needs for both dependence and independence create lots of inner conflicts for them and complicate their marriage. We usually get married to relieve our loneliness. We like to depend on a partner to make our lives easier. Yet, many relationships, nowadays, make us feel the ultimate sense of loneliness and desperation, since we feel the difficulty of relating to another person properly, and because we had imagined we could do all that rather easily, mostly on the power of love alone. Most of us had never felt so helpless psychologically when we had been living alone. We are terribly disappointed after many years of daydreaming about finding a partner to complete us. Thus, relying on our partners to cure our psychological needs is rather unreasonable and an irrelevant (ideal) expectation to set for our marriages.

In fact, a big hurdle is that even if our partners could satisfy our need for dependence, we personally sabotage their efforts by our naïve expressions of individualism and independence. Our false pride stops us from expressing our innate need for dependence and our partner's regular support directly. Instead, we pretend tenaciously to be emotionally self-reliant and tough. After all, showing neediness could tilt the balance of power in a marriage. Meanwhile, we try to fulfil both our dependence and independence needs just by playing some phony, idiotic roles and expecting our partners to realize their meanings and also respond favourably. Yet, these conflicting (unexpressed) expectations and awkward role-playing merely confuse and frustrate our partners, too.

Ironically, hiding our neediness to protect our pride cannot really help us and our relationships, either! Only by sharing our emotions we can boost communication at least, if partners are mature enough to grasp marriage purposes and do not take advantage of each other's vulnerability.

Since our emphasis, nowadays, is placed on individualism and independence, we should adjust our expectations from relationships accordingly. That is, **we should emphasize on independence and assume that relationships are no longer capable of satisfying our need for dependence *at a desired level.*** We must also prepare ourselves to deal with our inner conflicts (caused by inadequate dependence) without blaming our partners. Many readers might object: 'What is the point of being in a relationship, then, if partners cannot depend on each other fully?' This valid question is answered in this and other books in this series. However, the bottomline is that we cannot stress on independence so strongly and also seek dependence. This does not make sense. Therefore, dependence cannot be considered a legitimate relationship objective, nowadays.

At the same time, not fussing about dependence does not mean that partners do not advocate teamwork, compassion, and all the other good things that they must do together to make their relationship flourish. Showing compassion always helps the health of relationships when couples notice their partners' need for dependence despite their arrogant show of independence. It is a good gesture by partners to stay civilized towards each other in those circumstances. That is why MLove is an important purpose of relationships, nowadays—to make up for irreconcilable issues in relationships. However, when we keep switching erratically between our independence and dependence urges and roles in marriage, we must also expect that our partners lose their sensitivities and honest sympathies about our needs.

In our modern way of thinking, we accept open-mindedly that both dependence and independence are essential needs, and we naively believe we can cope with this big dilemma in our relationships. We often even assume that by some magical power we would find the right balance (between our needs for dependence and independence). We think we can make timely compromises so that both partners can fulfil their rotating needs for independence and dependence logically. This is an impractical expectation to set for relationships, although some mature couples can achieve it naturally.

This author's books, *The Nature of Love and Relationships,* and *Relationship Needs, Framework, and Models*, discuss the importance of relationship models for managing people's zeal for both dependence and independence. Basically, relationship models are developed, and chosen by couples, mostly based on the degree of dependence and independence that partners need and demand in a relationship.

Whether we like it or not, time has come for adjusting our assumptions about the conflicting needs of partners for both dependence and independence. It is time to stop the negative impact of these useless struggles on relationships. These facts should be clear to couples at the outset before getting married. This is necessary because, nowadays, the idea of 'dependence' has been losing its practicality in relationships. Thus, couples must think through and plan their relationships based on the assumption that they must remain independent in all respects regardless of their relationships' outcome. Hopefully, partners learn teamwork, MLove, and compromise, too, to make their relationships both manageable and wonderful. Yet, starting on the wrong foot, i.e., hoping that their need for dependency can be satisfied in a relationship, is simply opening the door for major disappointments. Overall, couples' awareness of these sad, growing weaknesses in modern relationships might help them think deeper and find means of mitigating their marital conflicts by becoming both realistic and more compassionate.

2. Financial Security is a rather obsolete concept, although one partner is usually the main breadwinner in relationships. The point is that financial security is no longer an automatic arrangement like the good old times. People are not getting into relationships for financial security anymore. Or at least they must not, as society is revolving around 'independence.' Now, financial security in relationships, when it happens, is by accident or some kind of agreement between partners. It is an exception, not an expectation. Financial security is no longer a norm or legitimate relationship objective, but rather a possible by-product of being in a relationship and only in the spirit of teamwork. Nowadays, partners should somehow understand and agree on the mechanism of their household finance before they commit themselves to a relationship.

3. SLove: Love can make couples' communication smoother and more effective. It also helps them satisfy their needs for compassion. Yet, love does not qualify as a legitimate general purpose for relationships, due to its illusive nature, especially the pure kind of love we feel towards our children, Nature, and sometimes for our artistic creations, i.e., SLove (selfless love).

We all like to taste love at least for starting a relationship, and love is a good gauge for measuring the degree of partners' attraction and success in fulfilling their sexual need. However, we should not consider love a reliable factor to keep partners together. Love cannot be an objective measure for assessing relationships, either. The reason is obvious. When we express love, we are influenced by a perception of Selfless love (SLove), while we are driven mostly by our Egos and love deficiency (ELove). We all have this spiritual need, SLove, to love someone or something passionately. When we meet a person who can stir this feeling in us, we consume ourselves with a perception of SLove. This individual becomes a mirage that satiates our need for SLove. At the same time, our need for ELove (ego-ridden deficiency love) further encourages us to identify this person as our soul mate. We are suddenly in love. This is great for bringing couples together. However, true SLove happens only rarely and only when partners are needless and enlightened persons. Therefore, our perception of SLove is only a transitory 'mood' and not a reality. ELove, on the other hand, is an absolute reality and not a perception.

Thus, ELove keeps placing more demands on partners every day, as its only purpose is to feed partners' selfish need for attention. It creates possessiveness, jealousy, and frustration.

Overall, love, as we express it so readily, nowadays, is not going to help relationships. Therefore, **we must remove love as a valid objective for relationships** (except for Mlove, as explained in the previous section about *Sensible Purposes.*) We can use 'love' as a gauge for attraction and for facilitating communication, but not as a factor of relationship success.

The arguments presented before regarding 'compassion' apply here, too. We all seek love too much, but do not know how to give love. Again, the supply and demand for love (all three kinds, i.e., SLove, ELove, and MLove) are unbalanced and causing undue pressure on our lives and society overall. We have become too needy for love since everything else in society is stressful. And we assume that by expressing love to someone, he/she gains the power or expertise to provide the genuine sympathy we need to mitigate social pressures.

4. ELove: (egotistic love) reflects the selfish need for love and attention and is mostly a reflection of insecurity. This type of love cannot be a legitimate purpose for relationships.

5. Trust: Sadly, mistrust is becoming a general condition in relationships, nowadays. Thus, trust cannot be a general, valid objective for relationships. Yet, partners must also stop fussing about it, and instead cope with some level of mistrust or doubts as long as the integrity of their relationship is not jeopardized.

6. Happiness: We expect relationships and our partners to bring us happiness, but they cannot. Whether we can capture happiness in relationships or not depends on a large number of factors, but mainly our mental capacities to interpret, absorb, and reflect happiness. Actually, relationship environments are normally too complex and demanding to induce happiness directly. Usually, if we are a happy person, we know how to generate our happiness within or without a relationship. The opposite is even truer. If we have no capacity for being happy, relationships normally make us unhappier. Thus, in all cases, happiness cannot be a legitimate purpose to impose on our relationships or partners. They cannot be responsible for our happiness or the lack of it. Couples should accept that the only likely source of happiness in relationships is the mere presence of a companion in their lives. If a partner's presence alone does not stir happiness automatically, the relationship has no other source of happiness to offer. Accordingly, couples must either learn to relate (at least passively) or opt for separation, but not nagging and demanding happiness.

Another misperception is that happiness is rather automatic in relationships at least due to its big potential to solve many of our personal problems, especially emotional and financial needs that we cannot handle alone. This is a false assumption and another illegitimate purpose to set for relationships in the new era. In fact, this mentality is destroying relationships and further reducing its capacity to cause even a slight measure of peace and comfort. Overall, expecting relationships to solve our problems is a damned objective. A good relationship helps us mentally to handle our personal problems more effectively, if we were smart and humble. A bad relationship, on the other hand, ruins our ability to even take care of our basic needs, let alone solve the complex problems of life and the relationship itself. Judging by the statistics, most relationships fail in the new era. Thus, instead of expecting them solve our problems, we should expect and prepare ourselves to face relationships' hardships, not to mention the high likelihood of separation. Relationships certainly become the source of new problems, instead of solving our existing conundrums. That is what this book, and the other books in this series are all about—trying to prepare the readers for the headaches of relationships. At the same time, this awareness can help smart partners perceive the purposes and potentials of relationships in a proper light, thus prevent its demise.

Playing more roles and games in hopes of pushing our partners to make us happy would not work, either. Although many experts advocate role-paying to make couples release their tensions and state the sources of their anxiety, this author believes that couples can decide about the viability of their relationships only by understanding the deep-rooted causes of relationship obstacles in the new era. Depending on partners' intelligence to learn the sad truth about relationships works better than keeping them hopeful by playing some artificial roles. This is particularly true when they are already under pressure mentally and physically. Role-playing causes more stress and frustration when partners feel the futility of their efforts deep down. Why they feel this way? From experience, we know that once the process of alienation between partners begins, it is almost impossible to return it to its initial state of moderate calm. The only thing that can save relationships is learning the truth about the real sources of problems, which often relate to partners' own irreparable idiosyncrasies.

7. Commitment: We have traditionally expected relationships to enforce a formal commitment for partners to stick together even when some aspects of their relationship are not ideal. Maybe 'commitment' was a useful tool in the past and even now. However, as a practical step, partners should recognize that, nowadays, the sense of commitment is vastly eroded by the need for individualism. Now, people insist on enjoying their lives at the highest level possible. They get out of their relationships sometimes even based on childish reasons or their perceptions of a better life with a different partner. The bottomline is that commitment can no longer be considered a legitimate purpose for relationships in the new era. Period.

8. Longevity: The above arguments used for 'commitment' applies to longevity, too. It was a practical purpose in the past, but not anymore. The main emerging relationship trends listed below show why longevity is a doomed expectation.

Table 1.1: Emerging Relationship Trends

1. Nowadays, most people do not seek a partner to merely satisfy their companionship need. Rather, they want their relationships make them happy and also satisfy a host of their needs and/or solve their personal problems. Thus, they usually blame their relationships for their personal failure to figure out life or find happiness. Meanwhile, couples are going through a painful, confusing transition period.
2. Greed and Ego do not disappear even when couples happen to be in love. In fact, people's growing drive for individualism and equality would boost their greed and Ego, which in turn reinforce their other pressing needs in relationships, including their needs for identity, control, recognition, retaliation, and love. The point is that love would not eliminate greed and Ego and all the subsequent problems they create in relationships.
3. People are forced to play games and roles all their lives. They are dragged into situations beyond their control to play along with others and assert themselves. This condition also infects relationships, as partners constantly play games and roles—out of necessity, sadly. Hardly anybody is natural these days.
4. Couples play games and roles to: 1) impress (charm), 2) flatter, 3) intimidate, or 4) snub each other. Therefore, the amount of time they are natural and sincere is too little.
5. Personal idiosyncrasies and insecurities have skyrocketed as social values have deteriorated, and vice versa. This vicious cycle would soon spin out of control and make the success of relationships less likely every year.
6. The chance of finding even a sane, reliable companion is very slim, let alone a soul mate. Yet, we have difficulty accepting this fact, as we want to stay positive. Our romantic search for a soul mate is preventing us from perceiving relationships and facing life realistically as an independent, self-reliant person.
7. For keeping an acceptable companion (let alone a soul mate), partners must have many common interests and compatibility, be good humans, understand relationships' basic, unique needs

these days, and know how to work on their relationship needs continuously. However, human nature does not support these requirements. In fact, our new social values make people more arrogant and needy every day, while human nature's impurity rises (and becomes more evident and irritating), too.

8. Most often, partners actually destroy each other's lives instead of enriching it. This is because life is getting more complex and stressful every year, people have more difficulty coping with social pressures, and they live longer, too. The outcome of this condition is that people are too disturbed and impatient to deal with their excessive relationship demands effectively.
9. Considering the above facts and many other reasons explained in this book, marriage should now be viewed as a temporary arrangement, unless both partners acquire all the high qualities required for building an effective relationship.
10. To attain relative tranquility, we must know the art of living independently instead of looking for a soul mate to bring us happiness. For all practical purposes, we must learn to live alone (in the sense of fulfilling our financial and emotional needs personally) instead of looking for relief in relationships.
11. We will always face a major trade off in relationships: They would always bring us big headaches, whereas for tranquility, we must deal with loneliness and be self-reliant. The dilemma is to make a right decision according to one's personality.
12. Our only hope is to develop a half dozen or so relationship models that fit couples' varied personalities and needs in line with current social values and couples' mentality. The goal is to provide a relatively tranquil atmosphere for teamwork and effective companionship. This book suggests that merely by developing and propagating a relationship framework and its corresponding principles we can achieve this goal. That is the only way to bring some objectivity back into relationships.

CHAPTER TWO
Marital Success Factors

We can identify the main success factors for relationships based on Chapter One's discussions of sensible and irrelevant relationship purposes. Marriage purposes and success factors are closely related concepts, but are not the same things. That is, we must understand, and set our expectations for, the right *purposes of relationships*, before getting married. Then, we must work actively on *success factors* to make our marriages flourish beyond its basic merits.

Actually, we can develop two lists based on sensible and irrelevant relationship purposes discussed in the last chapter: 1) A list of success factors based on the sensible relationship purposes, and 2) A list of conflicting factors and motives that preoccupy partners and taint their joint decisions. For a marital commitment (compared with mere cohabitation), partners must be more serious about their compatibility and knack regarding both the success and conflicting factors suggested below.

Success Factors in Marriage

First, we must recognize that three major objectives exist for marriage outside the innate need to mate, have a family, and face life's hardships easier. These goals (motives) maximize the interests and welfare of two intelligent individuals who view marriage as an institution or partnership. Thus, couples must try to fulfil these goals simultaneously for making their marriages successful. These goals are explained in general in this chapter, and then their elements are reviewed in the next chapter along with partners' compatibility measurement.

1. Increase Life Enjoyment: Marriage offers the opportunity to explore life jointly in a more significant manner. Obviously, sex, love, and compassion are expected to prevail and provide enjoyment, especially during the early stages of our lives when we need all those good things the most. More crucial, however, is partners' ability to share their life experiences in general and do certain activities together, which intensifies partners' enjoyment of life extensively. Life's inherent values become more vivid and meaningful when they are explored and appreciated jointly, while partners express and share their feelings and interpretations. Just the mere opportunity to have someone around to discuss, or complain about, life and social issues gives couples a warm sense of relief if not enjoyment. Married individuals have a longer life expectancy, since they can share their joys and anguish. They get a chance to share their hurts, mitigate the effects of external pressures on them, and get back into happy mood cycles faster.

2. Support and Cooperation: Marriage must offer a suitable environment for cooperation and teamwork to solve problems, and to strive for higher personal achievements. Partners' joint participation in household and family affairs leads to better results and a higher synergy with less energy wasted by each partner. More importantly, partners are expected to support each other functionally and psychologically in order to grow, think clearer, and stimulate a variety of communications that would be creative and thought provoking.

3. Sensible Commitment: The ultimate purpose of marriage is companionship. However, while 'companionship' remains a romantic and natural notion, 'marriage' feels like a contractual obligation of partners for a joint venture. We do not think and feel as much romance when we talk about marriage, as it is inherent in the meaning and purpose of companionship. This subtle expectation of romance fading with marriage is, of course, a realistic vision based on what we subconsciously know and observe in most marriages. Our bad experiences and general observations in society have given us a dubious view of marriage. It seems, particularly, that men are more reluctant to commit themselves to marriage, partially to protect their independence and partially due to their higher apprehension about married life and its inevitable anguish—perhaps because they have less maternal incentives that goad women more naturally and forcefully.

It seems as if with marriage we expect the innate purpose of companionship lose its steam eventually in spite of partners' immense initial love and romanticism. Accordingly, marriage seems like a scheme to keep partners together even under situations not tolerated in a non-committal companionship. Although we are not naive to assume that alienation problems can be resolved by making separation hard through marriage arrangement, we believe that some simple formalities (like the ones we now have) can protect us from situations where our agitated Egos explode and goad us make hasty and regrettable decisions. Through marriage, we are forced to see and practice some commonsense in making our relationships work, instead of searching for an ideal mate forever. After all, ideal couples can be found only in fairy tales. Nowadays, however, couples are unaware of, or ignore, even this basic purpose of marriage, i.e., a sensible commitment.

In marriage, we may eventually learn that stubbornness and false pride only lead to alienation and separation. We expect the loss of some intensity and passion in companionship over time, but hope to acquire the wisdom of comradeship to accept and adjust to our partners' imperfections. These imperfections would have separated partners if they were not married or had not learnt the means of curbing their obstinacy and false pride.

Accordingly, a special purpose in marriage distinguishes it from a simple companionship. We might call this a 'sensible commitment' to make a relationship work when it is logically possible. However, most of us are not familiar with this basic purpose of marriage (a success factor), or do not work on it consciously as a major requirement of marriage. Contrary to full commitment that many naïve partners dream and expect from their marriages, 'sensible commitment' is conditional upon partners' abilities to relate in many respects *in order to develop* a natural sense of commitment when hardships or conflicts emerge. The sensible commitment grows naturally when partners learn to relate calmly and respectfully, instead of expecting a blind commitment egotistically. Our view and concept of marriage is an incomplete picture, which we have learned from our parents and movies. We have never had an opportunity to grasp the real purposes (and shortcomings) of marriage before we get into one. And once we are in it, we do not know how to assess and respond to complex situations prevalent in modern relationships. We either suffer through it too much too long helplessly or run away from it prematurely, based on our emotional and arbitrary criteria for tolerance.

Conflicting Factors in Marriage

The most pervasive conflicting factors for marriage in the new era are noted below. They should be avoided at all cost:

1. Love Need: This is a strong and beautiful need that we crave forever, but often at the expense of a lifetime misery and disappointment. Everybody is misled by mushy movies that show how love makes people's life eternally beautiful and happy. 'Love need' occurs in three ways and waves. First, we crave being loved per se, like a deep psychological deficiency. Second, we imagine and believe that we adore a particular person and cannot live without him/her. Third, we build an image of love superficially in response to the sentiments that we believe a person is offering us, which we usually accept out of loneliness, desperation, or our innate urge to love or be loved—and thus we replicate the feeling of love. Yet, none of these love criteria is directly relevant for building a serious relationship.

Therefore, while we are trained to believe love is the main factor for the success of relationships, we must now turn 180 degrees and accept that it is not—just to focus on true success factors. Still, we learn and use Mlove to enrich or marriages.

2. Security and Dependence: The old assumption about the capacity of relationships to fulfil our needs for security and dependence is no longer valid in the new era. Accordingly, the main point stressed here is that we should no longer gauge the value of our marriages based on the level of dependence and security it can provide. They are useful features to develop in relationships, but their absence must not reflect on the viability and success of relationships. Craving security and dependence are against the basic principles of self-reliance and self-image that we value so much these days. Starting a partnership in a weak position would not help the marriage in the long run. The absence of self-image and innate personal security puts demands on both partners. The spouse who requires special attention and a sense of security would most likely become disappointed after marriage to find out that his/her spouse does not care or cannot offer the extreme attention that is demanded of him/her. The spouse pressed for special attention eventually gets fed up with his/her partner's abnormal demand, nagging, and withdrawals from the relationship.

The success of relationships, nowadays, depends largely on the personal strengths of partners and their abilities to increase synergy in their relationship, instead of being a needy person.

3. Financial Gain: It is needless to discuss the immorality and irrationality of planning personal gains as a decision factor in a marriage or companionship. Yet, many partners bring their calculating nature to relationships, nowadays.

4. Convenience: One or both partners may consider marriage a means or matter of convenience, financially or emotionally. Sometimes they do it just for changing their monotonous life routines. Family and cultural pressures to build a family lead to these types of marriages, too. Marriage is perceived as a scapegoat, while partners remain oblivious of its enormous potential for causing major headaches, inconveniences, and frustration of its own, instead of solving their initial problems. Focusing on personal problems and inconveniences, which partners hope to eliminate through marriage, usually reflects their ignorance of relationships' peculiar needs and capacity in the new era.

Knowing the success and conflicting factors in relationships, the next challenge is to find means of pinpointing and gauging them when we meet a prospective partner. Thus, the details of marital success factors are discussed in the next chapter, while we get cautious about the conflicting factors. In fact, the whole point for setting and measuring couples' compatibility should be to evaluate their relationships' chance of success based on proper factors noted in this chapter. Merely checking partners' compatibility in terms of sharing some traits—as is common nowadays—does not guarantee that their relationship would be successful. Instead, we must measure each partner's ability to focus on, and practice, particular success factors in order to enrich his or her marital relationship.

CHAPTER THREE
Couples' Compatibility

The following list of compatibility measures is developed based on last chapter's discussion of Marital Success Factors to help prospective partners gauge their relationship's strengths before getting married. These compatibility measures (success factors) are reviewed in this chapter.

Table 3.1: Compatibility Measures (Relationships Success Factors)
1. Compatibility to increase life enjoyments • General attraction • Communication and negotiation abilities • Activities and thoughts to share
2. Compatibility for support and cooperation • Teamwork • Support to pursue personal goals • Functional and psychological support • Joint problem solving capabilities • Knack for financial stability
3. Compatibility for a sensible commitment • Patience and Flexibility • Forgiveness • Dealing with anger • Compassion • Awareness of commitment • Expressing personal expectations

Partners' personality attributes and their capacities to fulfil the three main marital goals (increase life enjoyment, support and cooperation, and sensible commitment) offer relatively good measures of their compatibility. By assessing these success factors, we can estimate two people's abilities to relate without inflicting too much harm on each other. However, finding compatible partners is becoming harder every year due to the rising complexity of personalities and social values, as well as partners' naiveté about the real success factors in relationships in the new era. Instead, partners only put more demands on each other and raise their expectations from their relationships.

1. Compatibility to Increase Life Enjoyments

An implied expectation, when two individuals join, is to create synergy in all respects, including an enhancement in their life enjoyments above the levels that people can attain personally. If partners cannot deliver what is needed to achieve this added mutual enjoyment, the goal of marriage becomes questionable. Partners begin to doubt the value of staying in such a lousy relationship. Therefore, a few main factors that contribute to partners' increased life enjoyments are discussed below.

General Attraction

Obviously, general attraction brings two individuals together quickly and provides a great foundation for building all other aspects of a joint life. It simply reflects our needs for sex, love, and companionship, without the extreme implications of being in love or craving it. General attraction is a positive feeling of intimacy with our partner both physically and mentally. It is an authentic connection and friendship between partners, rather than a flimsy infatuation. However, this general attraction stirs teamwork, while partners fulfil each other's need for love and sex naturally. It also encourages partners to learn flexibility, patience, and tolerance, whereas without such attraction they would feel trapped or opt for separation and divorce with the smallest disappointment.

Communication and Negotiation Abilities

The compatibility of partners' personal values and philosophy of life is important for increasing their life enjoyment, but their abilities to communicate their viewpoints effectively are even more essential for raising their life enjoyments. They should be flexible, articulate, and patient, rather than hyperactive, dogmatic, and opinionated. They must be able to express their feelings and needs calmly without getting into quarrels, or withdrawing quickly because their communication feels futile or frustrating, e.g., when they fail to manipulate their partner perhaps. In all, a major test of compatibility is to find out how intelligently and calmly partners can discuss various issues. Ability to negotiate and be assertive is crucial for keeping the communication channels open and productive. Conversely, emotional reactions and oversensitivity prevent partners from finding their common interests even when they have some. Without proper communication, exploring common grounds and compatibilities, to increase their life enjoyments, becomes difficult. It would feel as if partners were highly incompatible when in fact both partners might have enough high personal qualities to share a happy life.

Communication plays a wide range of roles for relating, team playing, sharing experiences, psychological relief, etc. Thus, it is a crucial factor for raising partners' life enjoyments. Fortunately, the quality of communication is rather easy to measure if we look for the right clues actively.

Most communication problems emerge when one partner becomes the sole (or main) communicator prior to marriage. Partner 'B' agrees with, or simply absorbs, whatever 'A' says without expressing enough personal opinions. Therefore, 'A' believes 'B' is in agreement with him/her and his/her views, which gratifies A's egoism and sense of control. In reality, though, this is merely a sign of potential problems waiting for future explosions.

Partner B's seeming passivity may have several reasons. S/he may disagree with everything or most of what 'A' says, but holds back his/her comments because s/he does not want to contradict 'A' and jeopardize their relationship. Or s/he may be dominated by 'A' and does not *yet* know how to correct the situation and be assertive. Or, s/he does not have any special ideas to contribute to their communication, thus s/he remains simply content with this one way communication, at least for now. Thus, an incomplete, stressful communication process prevails between partners.

Then, after marriage, the timid (or passive/aggressive) 'B' makes his/her abrupt entrance with a new tactic as an overly active/aggressive partner. S/he makes her voice heard to make up for all the past inhibitions, and also because s/he does not know a better method of communicating, so in most cases she appears harsh and rebellious. Even if there were a slim chance that 'B' does not rebel, 'A' would eventually feel the void and the lack of intellectual communication with his/her partner, especially when his/her attempts to communicate are blocked by passive aggression and retaliation. An Ego driven partner (maybe egomaniac 'A') often dominates their communication and relationship too much. Conversely, a Model (maybe 'B') tries to accommodate his/her partner by agreeing with his/her viewpoints and even encouraging his/her way of thinking. Eventually, however, both partners feel lost and dissatisfied with this meaningless way of communication and its results. Especially, Model (maybe 'B') who merely listens in the first phase usually rebels or withdraws at last, leaving 'A' totally in shock and rejected.

Life enjoyments stem from good communication and calm exchanges of valuable thoughts. If partners are incapable of stirring inspiring chitchats, they eventually look for it elsewhere. Therefore, prospective marriage partners must know what real communication entails and ensure that theirs is enriching and stimulating enough at their intelligence levels. People need good communication skills in order to relate effectively. Yet, another crucial role of communication is to increase partners' enjoyment in life.

We can evaluate our communication abilities easily. If communication is dominated by one person, if partners always end up fighting and withdrawing, if one or both partners are not able or willing to express themselves and are secretive or ignorant, or if a partner is deliberately only a listener, most likely there would never be a reliable, healthy communication between partners. Communication is obviously the main cause of relationship failures, due to its crucial role for cooperation, relating, sharing experiences, peace, increasing partners' life enjoyments, etc.

A sign of a good communication is that partners equally and enthusiastically share their thoughts, get into arguments without ending in fights or withdrawals, find peaceful ways of compromising from time to time, and know how to negotiate for achieving satisfactory and productive results. They look for win-win solutions, instead of being competitive. Occasional fights and temporary withdrawals most likely erupt between these couples, too, but the frequency is negligible compared to those couples who almost always get into trouble every time they attempt to communicate, or when nothing comes out of their communication.

Activities and Thoughts to Share

Without high compatibility in lifestyle and thoughts, marriage would be a never-ending cycle of burning rage and freezing apathy—fights and withdrawals. Partners must have common thoughts to share regularly, especially on personal topics such as hobbies, self-awareness, life values and philosophy, social and political issues, etc. They should enjoy their discussions per se, rather than doing it randomly merely out of necessity, mostly for solving their growing problems.

While enhancing their life enjoyments through sharing of their *thoughts*, partners must also share certain activities and look for ways of appreciating the aesthetic values of life and Nature. If they do not have good compatibility in *things* they like, and like to do, at best they end up doing mostly their own things, while missing the basic joys of sharing activities and thoughts, as inherent human needs.

Many people have bizarre needs or insecurities that reduce their chance of compatibility with others. For an artist who finds special values in art and Nature, for example, living with a partner who is indifferent about these experiences would be tough and lonesome, especially if his/her partner does not have enough things to do him/herself, which would then often lead to more nagging. Of course, partners need not appreciate everything equally all the time as long as they have enough thoughts to share and things to do together without partners losing their independence or feeling pressured for attention.

Most couples get into quarrels due to their perceptions about inadequate attention, differences in tastes about food, the house they like to buy, outdoor activities, common friends, and other basic things that nobody could have imagined would cause so much friction after marriage. Obviously, partners would never agree on everything. That is why an effective communication is necessary for discussing their opinions and differences calmly. With good communication, some of their conflicts due to inadequate attention or common activities can be resolved. They learn how to make the best of their times together for sharing at least some thoughts and activities, while they give each other ample space for independence.

One way of testing and measuring this compatibility is to prepare a list of major interests and activities that partners like to do alone or share together, without trying to influence, judge, or ridicule each other's tastes and preferences. Of course, some of these interests must have become obvious during the initial courtship without a need to prepare a list. Yet, making a list together indicates the seriousness of the activities and interests as part of their life plans and not only during a short period. The list must contain only the items they regularly do and are sincere about, and not their dreams. Simple things, such as a long stroll in Nature, athletic endeavours, artistic explorations, reading and discussing a book, and gardening are some good factors for measuring partners' compatibility. Then, they can sit back and decide how they can fulfil those needs (their own and their partner's), without compromising too much just to make their partner happy. And they should stop assuming they can gradually make their partner understand and enjoy sharing the same activities.

Thus, the first set of compatibility factors (for increasing life enjoyments) entails, i) General attraction, ii) communication method and content, and iii) major thoughts and activities that partners can share. Together, these factors enhance their life enjoyments.

2. Compatibility for Support and Cooperation

The second set of compatibility factors entails the elements of support and cooperation in 'family,' which requires partners' goodwill and conscious efforts. Obviously, couples have the intention of cooperating and supporting each other in order to achieve common family objectives as well as their personal goals. However, they hardly know how to go about doing it.

Everybody has some vague ideas about marital obligations and duties. However, support and cooperation are much broader concepts that have lost their meanings in marriages in modern societies. Our showy needs for individualism and equality have eradicated all those good family values (i.e., obligations and responsibilities) that prevailed in old cultures. Thus, partners must now measure, at the outset, their own and their partner's compatibility factors for support and cooperation, e.g., one's capacity for teamwork and compassion, instead of relying on their implied intentions and promises.

Raising children is still the most basic and natural intention (rightly or wrongly!) for building a family. Children are our only creations with such complexity in physical and mental capabilities and delicate souls, too. This exalting creation that we so casually view as our common objective in marriage is developed in response to our instinctual need and intention for cooperation and support. Without a mutually strong sense of compassion, cooperation, and support, even this basic objective remains invalid and cannot bear fruit. Raising a healthy child requires smart parents. Humans have innate needs to exchange love, compassion, support, and cooperation with someone they trust in order to achieve and share better things in life. Partners must be capable of looking up to each other to play their roles effectively in their marital relationship.

Some of the factors related to this category of compatibility are discussed in the following pages.

Teamwork

Partners' knack for teamwork is the first factor to gauge for 'support and cooperation' compatibility. Teamwork deficiency is both a symptom of personal negligence and bad universal training. Nowadays, the economy and competition influence our mentalities and attitudes too much. The main lesson we learn at home, at school, and in society is to compete and win in order to prove our identities. Our value as a person is mostly judged by our superiority over others. In professional sports, our physical abilities and competitiveness lead to outrageous levels of compensation. Our children want to be like so and so basketball or hockey player in order to be rich. Competition defines the whole purpose and structure of organizations. In our jobs, we get involved with ruthless strategies to defeat our company's competitors, and we get into competition with our colleagues and bosses, too, for higher positions and rewards. In all, competition is evident and encouraged in everything we do. Thus, we sacrifice compassion for competition. This crude mentality is not limited to socioeconomic settings. Family life has become equally contaminated by this evil as well.

Instead of teamwork, marriage partners now appear more in competition with each other in all respects. They compete at home with the same tactics, mentality, and personality aspects they apply for outside competitions. They compete to acquire the power and status in family, as if it were another heartless entity to capture and control. Another major factor hindering teamwork is people's obsession, nowadays, to gain and stress on 'individualism,' without really knowing its true meaning. They perceive and express it in a demented way merely by becoming more selfish and aggressive.

Marriage partners fight to set their territories and force their viewpoints. They struggle to dominate the situations and each other. They compete for the love and respect of their children, while strive to impose their own ways and wisdom with them. They compete by struggling to prove that they work harder, deserve more, are more hurt, make more money, know more, are always right, etc. Thus, their simplest disagreement turns into endless quarrels, retaliations, or desperate submission of one partner. Children soon learn who runs the household, has the ultimate power to dictate their lives' direction and overrule their whims.

Overall, despite widespread propagandas in organizations and society, teamwork has found very little application in our lives. The pretences and talks of teamwork may deceive us to think that perhaps we can finally tame our dogged Egos and harmonize our intentions regardless of our personal interests. Alas, the competition, as the core of our social values, has also inflicted our family lives and is preventing teamwork. Instead, competition has been ruining the sense of teamwork and trust.

All this negligence is happening when partners actually need teamwork to support each other's aspirations more than ever and to spread good family values. Putting partners' personal goals ahead of family objectives would simply minimize their chances for compatibility in support and cooperation.

Still, we can try to gauge the intensity of our companion's competitiveness and domineering attitude, instead of expecting to find a perfect team player. Like all other human deficiencies, partners' obsession for competition and control in family life emerges at different degrees. We can measure our partner's teamwork capacity from his/her reaction to losing in a game; or when s/he has a choice for collaboration or competition. We can design situations and games to measure our partner's egoism turning into rivalry in everything s/he does. Then, we can take the same tests ourselves and determine how good a team player we are!

We fail to create a teamwork attitude and environment also because we always insist on being *right* about everything, and to prove our partner *wrong*. We must have the last word about everything and we are sure we know the best for everybody. This rude attitude becomes mostly evident after marriage when partners feel less obliged to impress each other by humble and gentle behaviour. Just to use an anecdote, a couple (J. and M.) often used to joke sarcastically about a global reality, perhaps in a rather exaggerated tone for fun. J. said that prior to their marriage, M. had kept telling J., "You are right," regularly. But right after marriage, M. had said, "You are wrong," over the first comment J. had made!

"I've not been right about anything since," J. whined with a sigh! Regardless of the apparent exaggeration and humour of this anecdote, at least it demonstrates the ironic truth about the dramatic change in relationships after marriage.

As a basic test to gauge their teamwork capacities, partners can discuss both their 'common' goals and personal ambitions before marriage and learn how they are planning to go about them and what those goals really mean behind the surface.

Support of Personal Goals

While teamwork is essential for fulfilling relationship goals and household responsibilities, partners' personal goals should also receive high attention. Partners should demonstrate their interests and abilities to support each other in pursuing their life objectives. Initially, it is important that partners know their major personal objectives in life and discuss them seriously. The goal is to evaluate each other's true feelings and reactions about their life ambitions, which are usually left out in casual conversations. When personal aspirations are discussed a few times, especially if already pursuing those goals, the reactions and the potential for support can be witnessed and assessed. Yet, it is crucial to have real personal objectives rather than faking ideas (dreams) that partners are not serious about. We always think of new ideas and goals after marriage, too, which can be discussed as they develop to show our general interest to gain our partner's support, too. The point is to discuss our personal plans only when we feel serious about them.

Often, a partner has a vague idea, or perhaps even a strong desire, to pursue a special goal and mention it casually. Then, s/he neglects to pursue it because of his/her lack of motivation, perseverance, ability, or any other personal shortfall. Still, s/he uses marriage as an excuse, or blames his/her partner, for not pursuing his/her goals. S/he eventually believes in this horrible injustice even him/herself and insists that marriage and/or his/her partner had been the cause of his/her failure. Many family frictions arise because partners forget to discuss their personal goals seriously, but mention all kinds of lost dreams because of marriage. Usually when a partner does not have personal goals in life, s/he holds the other party responsible for his/her perceived or real failures. However, partners should realize that if they let marriage stop them from pursuing their goals, they should only blame themselves. If we do not envision our aspirations seriously before marriage or do not get the stamina or motivation to pursue them after marriage, our partner must not be used as a scapegoat. If we make mistakes, or get caught in unpleasant situations contrary to our plans, we could blame our destiny or personal negligence, but making false claims or blaming our partner for our failures only reflects our poor character and immaturity.

Another cautionary point is that if one partner has lower needs and aspirations than the other, s/he would often *try* hard to bring down his/her partner's aspirations equally to the same level as his/hers, instead of making an effort to catch up with him/her. One partner's lack of life philosophy or aspirations damages the lives of both. Similarly troublesome would be when one partner's life philosophy and aspirations are outside the popular social norms, while the other partner basks in the mainstream values.

Functional and Psychological Support

Partners must assess each other's patience, compassion, and other relevant factors that reveal a person's mental stability and strength. A hyperactive, erratic, oversensitive partner is unable to manage even his/her own life, let alone being helpful to his/her partner during crisis. Partners must trust each other's psychological capacity to support their needs and goals before making the marriage decision. In addition, they should gauge their capacities to provide psychological and general support for small and big issues. This support helps relieve their stress of daily work and life challenges. It also stirs communication and strengthens the scope of their relationship.

Joint Problem Identifying and Solving

Along with partners' abilities to communicate, they must also be good in joint problem identifying and solving. This requires mutual grasp of each other's analytical approach and use of logic in assessing and addressing the situations and issues, finding practical solutions, and making rational compromises. Testing this ability is not difficult either. A hypothetical family problem or any story from the news can be raised along with some personal suggestions for a solution. We then wait for our partner's participation and suggestions for solving the problem at hand. We can assess our partner and the process after a few typical discussion sessions.

Knack for Financial Stability

Partners must have general knacks, plus joint compatibilities and responsibilities, for maintaining the financial stability of the family with solid plans and sense about their financial resources and expenditures. If they cannot work together and support each other to achieve their long-term finances, their relationship would be full of frictions and headaches.

The second group of compatibilities that we must seek in our marriage partner entails: i) teamwork for common objectives, ii) support to pursue personal goals, iii) ability to give mental and psychological support regularly, iv) joint problem solving capabilities, and v) knack for financial stability. Together, these four factors produce an environment of cooperation and support to nurture a friendly and constructive relationship.

3. Compatibility for Establishing a Sensible Commitment

History and experience clearly show that all the promises and vows we exchange at the wedding and all our good intentions when we join with our partner in matrimony are worthless. It is ironical that we still partake in this comical and hypocritical exercise by indulging such useless marriage rituals. When a couple is not compatible, life often becomes hell for them. Therefore, breaking their commitments and promises becomes the most natural and viable option for them. Some particular personal traits of partners can, however, make their intentions for commitments more realistic. Those traits would help them reconcile their problems easier, thus maintain a rather healthy marital relationship. The opposite is also true: Without these compatibility factors, the chance of marriage success is slim. It does not matter how much partners promise, or maybe even pretend, about making a compromise, they would not succeed without some natural sense of commitment instilled in their personalities.

Patience and Flexibility

Partners' ability to detect and tolerate their modest differences, rather than letting them turn into irreconcilable issues, is the backbone of all marriages. Without patience and flexibility, we break under the first wave of marital difficulties and decide to flee the stressful situation, instead of trying to find sensible solutions. However, most of us do not realize the need for high levels of patience and flexibility, nowadays, not as a personal sacrifice, but a harsh new reality in relationships. Most marital problems erupt, nowadays, from Ego clashes and struggles about who is right and who is stubborn. There are often no major problems and, in fact, partners may even like each other in spite of their raw personalities and ongoing frictions. Under these circumstances, false pride and stubbornness often goad partners to declare war and go for separation. Often, patience and flexibility (to override false pride and stubbornness) can help partners cool down initially, then come to some personal understanding of mutual problems eventually.

Managing Anger

Anger is a common, natural reaction. However, its level, what we do with it, and how much we can control it, is crucial. The ability to deal with anger is genetic and partly learnable. As a factor of compatibility, we should look for our partner's, as well as our own, ability to deal with anger. Usually anger erupts when either or both partners are highly opinionated, egotistical, and like to have the final say in everything all the time. Unless one partner does not mind being dominated by his/her partner, resistance and frictions lead to alienation and separation eventually.

Ability to Forgive

Another factor of compatibility is partners' genuine capacity to forgive, instead of being spiteful and reactionary. Naturally, when one partner makes a mistake, spite and retaliation would solve nothing. If the mistake is too harsh and hurtful to one partner and cannot really be forgiven even after a period of cool down, then perhaps not much is left to do but to seek separation. However, if the mistake is not really an intentional or major disappointment for the victimized partner, s/he must have the ability to forgive if they are both willing and able to learn something from this experience. Often, the victimized partner continues to live with his/her partner with the intention or thoughts of retaliation, which would only raise alienation and suffering for both partners. Thus, partners should measure their own and their partner's abilities to forgive and learn from their mistakes after a calm discussion about the causes of their conflicts and frictions. These abilities are not hard to observe and assess during the initial courtship.

Compassion

Partners' level of compassion is indirectly helpful in keeping them compatible. It is an important personality attribute that keeps our Egos under control. Actually, the ability to forgive, control anger, and exercise tolerance shows one's compassion and outlook on life in general. A sign of snobbery reflects low compassion, whereas some degree of humility, in conjunction with subtle confidence, can be an indication of tolerance and compassion. Prospective partners can (must) assess this factor rather easily as well during courtship.

Awareness of Commitment

Partners should make their business to fathom, and think of, commitment as a crucial part of marriage. We cannot think or make promises of commitment without really knowing its meaning, objective, and requirement. Only then we might actively look for the 'sensible commitment factors' that were discussed above to assess them in ourselves and our partners.

Expressing Personal Expectations

We should make it our business, from the outset, to share our expectations from our marriage frankly and seriously with our partner and insist that s/he does the same. It is important for partners to understand each other's major expectations from marriage, as well as their marital objectives, personal goals, and what they are willing to do, or not do, for keeping their relationship intact. They should gain this knowledge mostly in advance, before marriage, mainly indirectly.

Expressing their expectations honestly helps partners cross the bridge between *love* and *understanding*, while a bridge still exists to make this crossover possible. The difference between love and understanding is unknown to partners too often, and it remains unresolved before marriage. Partners believe they know each other already and that nothing would change their wonderful impressions of marriage afterwards. Therefore, they neglect to think practical because of their misperceptions of marriage. They naively think their partner would realize and respond to their expectations even better later automatically just because they are married. They think cohabitation or marriage would increase the level of mutual understanding and sensitivity, thus raising and resolving their expectations would be an easy routine after marriage. They might even believe that their grasp of each other's needs and expectations would be natural, thus unnecessary to discuss in advance. This wishful thinking is a natural, common feeling, but in reality it almost never happens. In fact, partners' level of understanding and responding to each other's expectations appears to decline fast after marriage.

The six personality attributes, i) patience and flexibility, ii) forgiveness, iii) handling anger, iv) compassion, v) awareness of commitment, and vi) expressing personal expectations make up the third set of compatibility measurements regarding the sensibility and strengths of partners' commitments to each other. If one or both partners are weak in many of these areas, soon alienation and frictions build up. Just making a marriage proposal or accepting it without serious consideration of the above points, along with partners' mutual acknowledgment of their importance, would be a big mistake. This process would take months to complete realistically—not a simple exercise to undertake quickly just to get married. The prevalent sloppy attitude, nowadays, merely leads to many years of agony and alienation before partners realize the need for separation and then face the hardships of divorce as well.

Personality Compatibility

Besides the compatibility (relationship success) factors listed above, partners' peculiar personality traits and eccentricities can help or hinder their relationship. In particular, the three personality aspects of individuals (i.e., Ego, Model, and Self) play major roles in the presentation of a person's personality and his/her ability to get along with others. In a nutshell, Ego accounts for a person's urge for security and fulfilling his/her aspirations; Model mostly reflects his/her adaptation ability and charisma; and Self is the level of love and spirituality s/he can access in the depth of his/her being.

Refined studies are necessary to establish how partners' three personality aspects may interact for optimizing their compatibility. Obviously, if both partners have strong Self orientation, they have the highest chance of compatibility and relating. Other than this least likely scenario, couples with moderate Ego and Model dominations could possibly relate within a certain relationship model, too. Thus, the idea is to explore the possibility of measuring the compatibilities of less perfect personalities within various likely relationship models. (Relationship models will be designed more explicitly in the near future. Yet, for a review of these models, this author's books, *Relationship Needs, Framework, and Models*, or *The Nature of Love and Relationships,* provide good insights.)

Ego and Model affect relationships extensively these days. Ego reflects mostly a demanding personality and Model is too needy. With a reasonable level of Model and Ego, people can usually get along fine. Only the excessive tendency in either or both Model and Ego makes a relationship intolerable. The other challenge is to determine which personality dominations of partners can possibly match, if at all. Is there any chance for people with relatively higher domineering Ego or Model to ever find a suitable relationship? We may not be able to find a definite answer before doing some detailed research. To be on the safe side, people must stay away from personalities with excessive Ego and Model dominations. These conditions make the chances of teamwork remote and most likely never lead to a healthy and productive relationship environment.

Nevertheless, partners must not only measure their Ego and Model intensity, but also determine partners' tolerance level required in relationships when Model and Ego are rather high. Presently, an accurate measurement of personality aspects in a person is difficult, however. This is due to not only the lack of a reliable method, but also people's proclivity to fake their personalities readily in the initial stages of their relationships.

Gauging people's personalities is hard when they misrepresent themselves intentionally or inadvertently.

Often, our personality characteristics are not apparent or known even to us. Yet, they reside deep in our unconscious awaiting an opportunity to surface with a bang. For example, it is possible that a partner's extreme sense of aggression and anger have been repressed within him/her for ages, perhaps due to domineering and abusive parents or a spouse. At some stage, these feelings may finally erupt in either an explosive or a gradual manner to reach an unbearable extreme. Childhood traumas erupt in a destructive form and most likely stay with the person for the rest of his/her life if something is not done about them. Nonetheless, most passive/aggressive individuals know how to falsify their personalities in order to confuse or attract others.

Although not everybody can measure the intensity of his/her or another person's personality aspects with a good degree of accuracy, s/he can still determine reasonably well how s/he stands on each aspect. Especially, if they are clever, they can do some quick tests to gauge the intensity of another person's Ego or Model. They should, in particular, measure each other's knack for financial stability to ensure they are compatible in terms of their approach and sense about money and spending their income. If they are incompatible in that regard, it is best to avoid that union on that ground alone. They might even choose to seek an impartial third person's opinion, which could be helpful. The mental guard that prospective marriage partners build towards each other is somewhat turned off or ineffective when they are with other people. Thus, an outsider can notice hints of personality aspects that two partners would not reveal to, or detect about, each other.

A more difficult problem arises when we naively force ourselves into a doomed relationship. For example, we might have a domineering Ego or Model, but do not know, care, or do anything about it. We hide our flaws long enough until we win the love of someone we like to marry, then release our real personality. In this case, we hurt ourselves as much as our partners by getting into a potentially doomed marriage. We may or may not ever find the motivation and opportunity to defeat our personality deficiencies. Yet, marrying somebody, if we have high Ego and Model tendencies, would only lead to long-term suffering mostly by ourselves. Unless we learn to become more rational and perhaps humbler, not getting into serious relationships is our best choice, especially considering the potential damage on innocent kids who end up facing their parents' animosity and fights. Yet, this is a high expectation to place on selfish people with huge Egos.

Is Compatibility Only a Wishful Thinking?

We may think that we can assess our partner casually based on things s/he does or says. Seldom do we make direct, designed efforts to measure the particular aspects of compatibility, such as a person's ability to solve problems or honour his/her words and commitments. This is partly because we do not know how, and partly because it is not a social norm yet, though we judge people hastily, anyway. While indirect and casual assessment has some value, it is not useful like a direct, designed test that we can actively develop and apply. These direct tests should be done in a stealthy, rather playful, manner when partners are not stressed or hostile. Customary casual assessments these days are based on our perfunctory judgments (and often hasty emotional justifications) of our partner's calculated actions and behaviours. S/he can lie or use Model to portray a different personality than s/he deeply is. In direct (but secretive) testing, however, we might develop situations and ask questions that disable Model to play a prominent role, and thus giving our partner's deeper personality attributes a chance to emerge.

A hurdle for gauging partners' compatibility lies in the fact that they mostly meet by accident, without any prior planning to look for certain qualities or even know what compatibility means for them. In fact, if we adhere to our rigid definition of compatibility factors, it seems that only personal perfections can guarantee compatibility. That is, only individuals with no or minimal psychological shortfalls, who are well aware of their needs and flaws and respect their partners' needs as well, can be compatible. The rest of us, who have psychological deficiency, are goaded by our Egos, and do not know what our partners or we need in terms of life enjoyment and support, have no opportunity of finding compatibility with anybody. We have no chance of having a peaceful life, because we can never be compatible with anybody, not even if our partners were perfect human beings. We ruin everything personally single-handedly because of our egoism and insecurities. In the final analysis, it seems as if our own shortfalls make every one of us incompatible with the rest of the world.

Nevertheless, seeking compatibility is a big challenge due to our idealism and high expectations. While we keep seeking an ideal partner without knowing how to gauge compatibility, no one can satisfy our needs. At the end, our own flaws make us incompatible with everybody else, anyway. These facts suggest that most of us are doomed to suffer of incompatibility syndrome all our lives, mostly by our own faults.

How can we accept such a harsh truth and admit our flaws? Someday, we may be able to find better ways of searching and matching people through well-crafted mechanisms rather than depending on accidents to bring couples together. Of course, we can rely on computer matchmaking only when (sometime in the future) we have done sufficient research and understand which personal flaws of couples are possibly sharable between them, if at all possible. We should learn how couples may be mutually tolerant of each other's unique idiosyncrasies. This tool can help less perfect people live together harmoniously, while staying vigilant about their moderate incompatibilities forever. A more challenging task, of course, is to find out how couples with severe incompatibilities can be helped, mainly psychologically for a rather acceptable joint life with minimal frictions and sufferings—or by designing and using a special relationship model along with some practical guidelines.

Unfortunately, not even professional help is available out there, nowadays, to measure partners' incompatibilities and give them at least a heads-up about their incompatibility levels and looming headaches. The basic tests in the market these days, which claim to detect partners' compatibility, are flawed and ineffective in terms of their designs. Yet, our persistence and preference to ignore even the basic clues or our own basic perceptions of incompatibility readily shows the low potency and value of our logic and the dangers of intuition these days. Still, most couples rely mostly on their intuitions, chemistry, and vain values that society and parents have injected into their minds regarding relationships' success factors. Perhaps sometime in the far future people finally find access to reliable compatibility tests to know where they stand and what kind of a relationship they might be able to build together. For now, even basic compatibility tests can assist couples pinpoint at least their incompatibilities and those areas of clear potential problem.

Besides the need for a basic compatibility, it is important to learn patience and acknowledge that our crude mentalities and humans' inherent faulty nature make it hard to develop even tolerable relationships. Society must also educate people about relationship needs, partners' compatibly factors, and useful guidelines for relating. Surely, the goal is not to help only fully compatible people marry. Rather, the objective is to empower most couples who feel attracted to each other develop a good relationship for themselves through education, self-awareness, compatibility tests, and choosing a proper relationship model.

Surely, compatibility testing is most useful before marriage in hopes of predicting the most likely outcome of a proposed relationship. It can help couples choose the right partner and relationship model for them. However, once the decision is made, couples should strive to make their relationship work in the best ways possible rather than whining and arguing with each other. Instead, they should now keep working actively on the success factors discussed in this chapter.

On the one hand, it is wise to postpone any marriage until partners have had a chance to overcome all their doubts about compatibility factors, general risks, and circumstances of their union, especially about partners' personalities. If, at the end of their thorough evaluation, they still have doubts about some aspects of their compatibility and their marriage's prospects, then most likely something is amiss. That kind of union would fail and partners would suffer in the process way beyond what they can predict at the outset.

On the other hand, couples must gauge the sources of their doubts. Many factors, including our natural (or keen) search for compatibility, our big expectations from marriage, and the necessity for partners' consensus on personal and joint goals, goad them not to accept anything less than close to perfection. Yet, this ideal is infeasible and not recommended here, either.

A full match and compatibility is unrealistic, after all. The idea is only to learn about the *practical* forms of compatibility for various relationship models that might be suitable for our unique situations. The goal is to gauge the level of personality discrepancy and potential for future headaches. If not enough compatibility exists, it is wise to stop, especially if partners cannot even agree on the essential factors for the success of a relationship. In particular, it is important to measure partners' compatibility factors for a specific 'relationship model' that seems most suitable for their mentalities and personal needs, especially for their desired level of personal independence. Nevertheless, prospective spouses must grasp the concepts of relationship models and choosing the right one for them.

A common mistake, which becomes evident only after marriage, is that one or both partners assume and perceive they are getting into a perfect, or at least a normal, marriage. After marriage, they seek, and insist on, the *perfection* they had imagined for a 'normal' relationship, and instead only get more disappointments, distress, fights, retaliations, and speedy alienation. The mirage of marriage becomes clear to them so late harshly. Partners must realize at the outset that most likely they are by far not a perfect match, but more importantly why and in what respects; and how they can possibly make their marriage work despite the known, and potentially a lot more, imperfections that usually surface later.

A *normal* relationship is filled with inconveniences and quarrels, far from our perceptions of perfection. We must also be careful with our personal definition of perfection. We often expect others to be perfect in the way we define perfection for our convenience and according to our personal values in life. In addition to this naïve demand, we allow ourselves to be and behave any way we like—allegedly perfect—again as it suits us. We look at the world and people for our conveniences, needs, interests, and out of pure selfishness.

Nonetheless, we must spend enough time to study certain crucial traits and attributes of our prospective partner patiently, instead of deciding hastily, either positively or negatively. In particular, we must try to imagine how we might learn to cope with some likely imperfections and incompatibilities. Despite all our love for a person, we must know realistically whether, and how well, we might tolerate specific irritants and small nuisances, which seem likely already, for many years to come without losing our sanity. Even small problems and irritants against our values might lead to divorce. Therefore, time for a right decision is now, before making a commitment, while also appreciating that no couple can be fully compatible!

CHAPTER FOUR
Marriage Decision

In the author's opinion, marriage is the second most critical decision, nowadays, in a normal life circumstance—*ironically* next to separation and divorce after to a long cohabitation. The process of deciding 'to marry or not to marry' a certain person is quite delicate and difficult, as we are not aware even of our own psychological needs and defects, and have no knowledge of our prospective partner's deep emotions and needs, either. We underestimate the complexities of marital life, due to our inexperience and naivety during the courting stage. Thus, we are unprepared to face marital demands and commitments. We know very little about relationships' specific needs and we do not know how to assess partners' unique personalities, needs, expectations, and common objectives. We do not know how to prepare ourselves for new challenges and changes in our lives.

Assessing Our Mood and Decision Criteria

We wish we had had foresight and wisdom regarding marital agonies always too late—only when marriage conundrums are overwhelming us and we are cursing the person who invented the notion of marriage. We recall the story of Adam and Eve's first meeting and remind ourselves of the tyrannical roots of relationships. Yet, almost all of us ignore assessing both our marriages and divorces logically and deeply enough.

We are simply naive about marital demands and difficult changes we must make in our mentalities, although maybe not the ones our spouses would like to impose upon us! All this would be contrary to our wonderful imaginations of marriage. The discussions in the first three chapters offer enough clues regarding the depth of marital conflicts and our naïve approach about marriage decision.

Thus, it sounds logical to assess our willingness and ability to change, since even marginal 'independence' would become a contentious expectation within our new identity as a spouse. Besides understanding the need for big personal adjustments, learning how to do it and why is also essential. We must refine our expectations and attitudes and learn to apply our Model (the personality aspect for coping) more than what we have been, or believed in, playing. We must learn to defeat the evil of domination and possessiveness in ourselves quickly, or else expect a life of fights and pains. If a person does not recognize and prepare for these facts, and the need for big changes, s/he must avoid marriage. Or, at least, get ready for a huge shock and lots of frustration probably for the rest of his/her life.

Unfortunately, most people make their marriage decisions rather impulsively, instead of systematically based on proper knowledge of relationship needs and demands. Usually couples court for years, while assessing each other and a marriage, too, based on odd, irrelevant factors. Yet, the final decision to get married usually happens within days, if not hours or minutes, with one partner proposing and the other accepting, and viola we have a *shoddy* commitment and a *risky* marriage. What happens at this moment to make such a vital decision is often unclear to those making and accepting the proposal, but it is usually a matter of sentimentality and a hasty, spontaneous response to a surge of swift personal urges and needs. The couple simply cannot live without each other all of a sudden!

Fine, but why marry before the issues discussed in this book are quite clear to them and discussed patiently? Peoples often imagine they have thought through their marriage option long enough already, maybe even for years, yet most likely they have not analysed the right factors realistically. Accordingly, partners' spontaneity and approach for a marriage decision is too risky, nowadays.

Instead of exchanging a marital proposal, partners should only decide if it is time to explore the possibility of marrying. If yes, assessing our decision criteria gets the highest priority. Surely, the peculiarities of a relationship should determine the outcome of the decision, only after partners have spent ample time to sort out all the angles. However, partners should know the right criteria for making a final decision. The present mode of marriage decisions is outdated and unsuitable for such a critical business. Indeed, marriage decisions should now be viewed and handled like a major treaty, which needs plenty of negotiating and planning. Furthermore, we should learn about potential marriage agonies on top of the hassles of divorce, which is a highly likely outcome of most marriages these days. This means the matter of learning about *'divorce' at the time of marriage* becomes essential, in particular.

In fact, we should learn to make our marriage and divorce decisions in a rather reverse order. That is, we must think and discuss divorce (consequences) at the time of marriage, and ponder and negotiate marriage (purposes) when contemplating divorce. We should use this proactive principle in evaluating our marriage and divorce decisions. The purpose and benefits of these radical decision criteria will be elaborated shortly. First, however, let us imagine partners' most likely reaction to this cynical proposal. Let us review the practicality of thinking about, and discussing, divorce at the time of marriage.

Naturally, discussing divorce sounds depressing and cynical when we are planning our wedding and all its related joyous events. We are timid to ponder or raise this insensitive issue, since we do not wish to spoil the entire romantic mood. We do not dare to taint even our own sense of love and joy, let alone suggesting the discussion of a topic with such cynical nature to our prospective partner. It is unromantic, for sure, and our beloved would resist listening to our seemingly negative and calculating thoughts, and then asking him/her to share his/her views, too! Nevertheless, those reactions and resistance are all part of the evaluation process as well. We would be labelled uncompassionate and paranoiac. Yet, allowing these thoughts prevent a proper evaluation would be our first error in marital life. If our views agitate our partners, the situation would offer a good opportunity to predict (and measure) his/her wisdom and attitude during tough times and use this information for our final decision. It is crucial to arouse, now, those hidden emotions that would definitely erupt later in marriage. In fact, it is quite wise to initiate the process of unravelling partners' thoughts about sensitive matters and examining their abilities to negotiate and compromise. All these issues would come out for discussion and dispute sooner or later, so why not sooner? The romantic mood we are trying so hard not to spoil subsides shortly after marriage, anyway. You can bet all your physical and mental assets on that!

Most of us hide foolishly behind our emotions and resist the truth we sense or hear about marital life. Yet, avoiding the truth would neither help us now with our decision regarding this serious commitment, nor change its outcome later. Marital realities and emotions always erupt so unexpectedly only after the fact like a volcanic mess. Thus, we are definitely better off to test the waters now. For example, if having a prenuptial agreement seems practical and necessary, we must not hesitate to discuss it with our partner merely on the ground that it might spoil the mood. Nevertheless, we should be careful with our interpretation of 'practical and necessary' and do not allow our timidity force us choose an optimistic position about the future of our marriage. On the contrary, always work from the worst-case scenario position.

But what do we mean by discussing divorce at the time of marriage? This sounds like a bizarre strategy to contemplate at the very least! However, the purpose of discussing divorce in advance is to appreciate the headaches of most likely scenario when divorce becomes inevitable. After all, this is a sad reality we should learn to cope with in modern societies. Thus, as a start, we should read books about the hassles and hardships of divorce, or getting trapped in unpleasant or lousy marriages. Too many marriages end up in this sad position, since partners do not have the nerve or resources to pursue other options or start all over with a new relationship subsequent to a divorce. Thus, by contemplating divorce, we like to do two important things, although a few other merits of following this strategy are discussed in the next section:

First, we study the most common repercussions of divorce on individuals emotionally, psychologically, physically, and financially in general. Many books and articles about divorce and its effects on individuals and their children are available. Some of those hardships are discussed in Part II of this book, too. This background would help a lot. The amount of time we invest on this education is the most justifiable and profitable project of our lives. The more time we spend on understanding the hassles of a bad marriage and divorce, the more time and money we save in life, even compared to the most profitable business venture we have ever done. Actually, if governments did their jobs properly and forced this essential education at high school, our brains would be familiar with these facts and decision criteria to a great extent already!

Second, we try to predict the potential causes and outcome of divorce based on our particular situation and personalities. We can imagine future events under most likely scenarios, and then project our position and reactions by considering our life ambitions and personality. Certainly, anticipating our feelings as a married person or after a divorce is tough, especially since our age and length of marriage would affect our feelings and positions a lot. Still, developing a preliminary impression of marriages' general pressures, as well as the devastating effects of divorce, is not impossible. Then, just try to multiply it ten folds to possibly gain a more realistic sense.

For example, we might learn that the feelings of loss and grief after divorce are many folds severer than the feelings of losing a mere companion, which we are most likely familiar with already. Regardless of the sense of love loss in 'marriage' and 'companionships,' the pain of unfulfilled commitments and dreams after divorce is many folds bleaker compared with a mere separation in a simple companionship. We learn that the sense of loneliness and failure after a marriage breakdown, or while enduring a flawed marriage, is often more suffocating than the loneliness we feel during bachelorhood when we have not yet basked in many years of marital life dependency and conveniences. The feelings of loneliness and failure intensify exponentially according to our age, too. If loneliness hurts now that you are young and crave independence, try to imagine the shock and anguish of separation after a long marital life.

During marriage, we gradually lose our zeal for autonomy as we get addicted to a new lifestyle slowly. We become much softer and more vulnerable to the loneliness feeling and state after many years of joint life. In a sense, it is often wiser to stay unmarried and keep our knack for self-reliance than marrying, becoming vulnerable, and then being left alone and confused. Reading books about 'coping with divorce' would show the immense level of distress and confusion that divorce causes. The anguish of loneliness is only one of divorce repercussions. We feel cheated and deprived out of a fruitful life. We feel like a real loser—lost, abused, unappreciated, misunderstood, and so much more. Most of us would, eventually, after a few months or years, overcome the primary feelings of loss and loneliness as we gain our sense of independence partially. Yet, we would always carry deep scars in our psyches for the rest of our lives.

The task of evaluating divorce scenarios is not easy, but most importantly it is not intended to cause apprehension and paranoia about marriage. We only want to make our marriage decision as educated as possible and be ready. And sadly, no knowledge is more relevant regarding marriage than divorce information. Next to a review of hypothetical divorce facts and scenarios, assessing partners' ambitions and characters at the present time is also productive. This assessment includes a thorough review of partners' assets and liabilities brought into this partnership, financially, emotionally, psychologically, and physically. This is the right time to measure partners' capacity, mostly in terms of their inherent compassion and intelligence, to share a joint life and relate.

Thinking divorce at the time of marriage is meant to be an educational process to prepare both partners for a productive relationship according to a viable relationship model, or stop them from making a mistake (i.e., marriage) that they would regret. No amount of time spent on this educational process—until partners are absolutely sure one way or other—is ever a waste. Ideally, they should **write** a proper agreement to reflect their initial efforts to make the right decision, but also recall all these conversations and promises. Many of these issues and agreements would help in preparing and signing a marriage contract. Two people can live together for as long as necessary to figure out these details and study each other's temperament, patience, compassion, etc. Then, if they wish, they can write the agreement and make their cohabitation official, if they truly think their marriage has some tangible benefits.

All these discussions of 'thinking divorce at the time of marriage' would become also handy for choosing a proper relationship model. Partners must understand the implications and requirements of relating within that type of environment (a particular relationship model) and learn about the factors that are essential for maintaining a relationship with minimal frictions. Partners' discussions also prepare them for raising and negotiating the topics that become most contentious when the possibility of divorce comes to fore in the future. At that point (when divorce seems inevitable), recalling their initial conversations and contract would prove most useful. It would be the best time to 'think of marriage at the time of divorce.' Divorce is discussed in detail in Part II. The newlyweds or those considering marriage are particularly encouraged to read all the chapters in Part II very carefully.

Marriage decisions should always follow an educational process and never be a spontaneous act (like an outburst of dormant emotions). The process must entail analyses and negotiations between partners until the details of their future relationship are examined and worked out in a fine plan in line with the **decision criteria** and **success factors** suggested in this book. It would be very much like gauging a joint venture, which is usually the true nature of marriages, nowadays. This process might take a week, a month, or more to complete, until partners are quite in sync with the details of their well-planned future relationship, perhaps even with a partnership agreement addressing all the issues raised in this book. At the end of this process, the marriage decision becomes clear naturally without the need for one partner proposing it spontaneously and the other feeling the need for a decision equally unprepared.

Developing a Partnership Agreement

We all live with strong senses of romanticism and hope. Yet, it is prudent to view marriage a risky business partnership, nowadays, besides a romantic adventure. Naturally, this sounds like a silly, cynical proposal to even ponder, let alone push on our beloved coldly. However, the sad truth is that the real life and marriage environment cannot be any further different from the image that most couples build from love stories and movies, nowadays. All the evidences from family relationships and divorce statistics show that marital life in modern societies turns into a contentious partnership, anyway, with couples fighting hard for their rights and equities. Spouses are adamant and alert regarding even their household activities being always distributed equally and fairly between them, let alone their financial issues. Therefore, with this mentality and reality in sight, maybe soon the society learns how to handle marriage practically like a *romantic business,* too!

Ironically, marriages now look like business partnerships that has been put together hastily without partners knowing much about the business they were getting into, their capitals and assets, and their shares of total equity, in case the business dissolves, etc. Of course, all other purposes of marriage are also crucial and will be discussed soon, too. Yet, we should begin our evaluation process with business factors, since, in the end, money always becomes a touchy issue, especially when partners get hostile near the divorce stage. Teaching these harsh realities of the 21st century at high schools is very important, so that the youths' mindsets are readily prepared for these new social facts.

In the absence of a better system, judicial systems follow the 50/50 asset distribution rule for most cases. Surely, this cannot be an equitable formula, since partners' income and initial assets can never be always equal. Many other sensitive financial issues, such as family budget, savings, investment decisions, and financial affairs play prominent roles in family life, nowadays, and create painful frictions, since they are not discussed and decided on at the outset. Then, after marriage, the more domineering and demanding partner begins subtle tactics, or maybe even nasty manoeuvres, to take charge of the affairs, with the other partner often losing his/her voice about most matters. All these contentious issues become the sources of arguments, conflicts, retaliations, and all kinds of nastiness that soon taint most relationships.

Perhaps standard marriage contracts will become available to the public soon, so that couples can only fill out some clauses and sign it. All the topics needing a discussion are also noted in an accompanying pamphlet to guide partners through premarital negotiation and mental preparation before making their decision. The process would feel easy and rather natural with no need for partners to think of the details themselves, but only follow the format and guidelines suggested in those upcoming standard contracts and accompanying pamphlets.

Two people can cohabit for as long as necessary to figure out these details and study each other's temperament, patience, etc. Learning about each other's personality for teamwork and negotiation is a crucial strategy for establishing the depth of items that require discussing in advance. Then, if they wish, they can even write the agreement and make their cohabitation official, if they really think their marriage has some tangible benefits for a long haul.

A big goal of 'marriage evaluation process' before wedding is to unravel major personality differences and high potentials for future clashes. This process is especially useful for alerting young partners about the highly likely marriage problems and getting themselves ready for both facing and preventing them rationally. It helps them learn about the tough (but crucial) relationship needs, especially for teamwork and financial sense. Predictable, touchy issues in modern marriages that couples are often ignorant about should be listed in standard contracts, so that they get a chance to ponder and learn. Even if a partner reneges on his/her written commitment or agreement, we still know that we had done our homework in communicating our fair expectations at the outset. If a marital relationship suffers, it would be due to new ideas and demands that a partner tries to impose on his/her partner. Normally, partners should not agree with each other's new proposals and demands, unless they look reasonable, in which case their agreement could be modified properly and formally if it is a serious matter. Still, partners must make sure they are not manipulated, which is sometimes hard to know, but usually cause additional marital conflicts and alienation.

These scrupulous steps are in line with the discussions in Part I about relevant marriage purposes and success factors.

Personal independence in marriage is jeopardized due to not only emotional issues, but also loss of basic control on financial and personal preferences. Arguments start about who should be responsible for what, whether all their income should go to a joint account, how, and who has the final say about expenditures versus savings, the kinds of investments, etc. All these matters need teamwork, mutual understanding, goodwill, faith, and most of all great communication skills. Negotiating and assertiveness before marriage can mitigate a *reasonable portion* of the arguments and aggressiveness that normally erupt after marriage. Especially, partners getting an opportunity to evaluate each other's knack for negotiations without getting nasty or testy would prove precious.

Then, partners must remember and honour their contracts, while they remain calm, assertive, objective, and willing to negotiate after marriage, too. One partner should not allow emotions and subtle tactics of the other partner influence him/her to forget his/her established rights before marriage. Loss of independence and financial controls often happens gradually when one partner finds the chance to abuse his/her partner's soft spots and take charge eventually. When the controlled partner feels these manoeuvres, s/he can either cope and suffer, or get into horrendous waves of fights and struggles, and then, most likely, go for separation.

Besides minimizing partners' power clashes, the main goal of partners' initial discussions and consent about a fair and friendly financial scheme is to secure their relative financial independence in general. Mixing their income, investments, bank accounts, etc. is not appropriate for the new era. In fact, the main features of this agreement should be ideally put in writing and signed by partners merely for remembering their commitments. Even better, serious and complex issues should be put in binding (standard) agreements to protect partners against future claims and demands.

The scheme is not meant to stir tight controls and measures for everything. The big idea is to keep personal independence and controls over one's financial decisions even after marriage. Partners would surely be generous towards each other without feeling obliged to account for what they do with their savings beyond what is agreed to for joint family expenses and capital purchases like a home, car, etc. The scheme should definitely be fair, flexible and friendly and treated as a financial plan for mutual understanding and consent. Clearly, when one partner does not work or have enough income for any reason, the other partner makes a higher financial contribution towards family expenses. However, partners should have their own savings and investments in general, while they could also have joint savings and investments if they both desire, but not as a marital mandate or dictated by one partner.

Discussing and possibly documenting each partner's share of duties and family roles, especially when children are born would not be a bad idea, either. These basic arrangements are not meant to be too strict like a treaty or constitution, either. Rather, they can be adjusted later by negotiation and goodwill. All we need to establish before marriage is a sense of mutual understanding and responsibility, financial structure, flexibility, comradeship, and good intentions. Above all, this process would help partners' grasp of each other's needs (now and in the future). It shows their negotiating skills and it lays out the foundation for a teamwork atmosphere that should prevail in a healthy relationship. Hopefully! Conversely, if prospective marriage partners do not see the need for these initial friendly negotiations, or discover big disparities in their needs, they have saved themselves the big hassle of marrying and arguing forever or opting for divorce. Ideally, they stop getting into a marriage that seems doomed already.

Then again, we cannot defeat humans' evil nature mixed with lots of mushy sentiments and rising lunacy! Thus, we should still be ready for the usual marital problems that often arise. The only thing any kind of premarital negotiation and agreement can do is:

To reduce the chances of early frictions after marriage, prevent big misunderstandings between partners, display partners' knacks for discussion and teamwork, and start with a more realistic sense about marriage. We should even expect many partners dishonour their agreements and claim they were fooled into signing them, even if a third party had explained and witnessed partners' words and intentions to them.

On the one hand, the notion of premarital negotiation or contract feels absurd! On the other hand, the idea of 'thinking divorce at the time marriage,' as a tool for anticipating and preparing for marital conflicts, makes so much more sense now after reflecting upon the intentions of this book's radical points, including even the loud idea of premarital negotiation and a written agreement!

Certainly, without some degree of faith and mutual trust between partners, they can write a ten-thousand-page contract and still see it violated after the marriage. Hoping partners stay rational, fair, and patient is naive and a good reason to doubt the value of the logical approaches suggested in this book. Still, for the same reasons, pondering all these precautionary measures before marriage appears to be our only chance for reducing our most likely future headaches. Meanwhile, all we can hope for is that someday soon we realize the need to be a bit more logical and practical about our marriages, mostly for own good.

A major marital problem arises when one partner notices a sudden change of position in the other partner. Especially, when partners do not talk about family budget, work, income, and other arrangements before marriage, the partner who has withheld his/her demands suddenly finds the courage and urge to parade his/her emotions and needs. This would not only feel like a change of personality, but also a sign of rebellion to the other partner. If partners have an opportunity to express their demands (which could in fact reflect their legitimate needs) at the time of creating their marriage agreements, the perception of personality change and new demands would less likely erupt and cause a big shock and friction between partners later.

Again, as stressed a few times already, finding the nerve to implement the thoughts and steps of preparing an agreement with our partner is a major task these days. Yet, this would become a natural and common practice in the near future, simply because it would both prevent those potentially doomed and risky marriages and reduce the common frictions that often emerge soon after marriage. At least a sizeable group of practical partners might start to prefer this approach to the merely romantic, sloppy means of marriage, nowadays, which usually leads to big headaches.

The whole point is that a little bit of time and controversy at the beginning, before marriage, would not only save tons of time and hassle during separations, but also strengthen their marriage. A judicial system should find ways to recognize and facilitate the process of preparation and legal documentation of a preliminary agreement for all marriages. They might do so if they realize that all the time and efforts partners might spend on negotiating and preparing a contract is fully justified. It saves a lot of time, money, divorces, and agony later for people and judicial systems. Especially, all the additional work before marriage when we are young is much more bearable than doing ten times more work and enduring the hassles of divorce when we are older and have less energy and patience.

Partners should really take their times initially when they are allegedly in love, calm, energetic, and collected, rather than pulling their own and each other's hairs during the stressful period of divorce as two mad, ferocious enemies.

Surely, seeing marriage as a *romantic business partnership* would appear ridiculous, insensitive, and impractical to us. When we feel love towards someone, swiftly our eyes, ears, and brains go on vacation and refuse to consider the simplest suggestions or words of wisdom, let alone bothering with business transactions that hinder the prospect of winning someone's heart. All those romantic feelings of love that we read in poetry books are true and apply to all of us to some degree. They fool us. When we believe we love somebody, we can give everything we have and sacrifice even ourselves just for having his/her love or even the mere honour of his/her company. Nothing else matters to us at that moment except being part of his/her life now, forget what may happen in a few years. When we are in love, we undermine the essential factors for a workable relationship and assume everything would work out nicely at the end. We naively believe love would solve all the problems, even if 'love' were one-sided. But in reality, the opposite is true: Peculiar marital problems and widespread personal idiosyncrasies kill even true mutual love very quickly. All those love stories in books and movies, as well as our own feelings of infatuation, are too misleading and untrue. This book's ideas are based on not just scientific facts and statistics, but also this author's several experiences in marital and love affairs and their agonizing outcomes. Still, none of these cautions would probably convince the youths to look at their love affairs more practically in line with the new era's realities!

Sadly (or luckily), no remedy for love and its traps exits. As long as we hear and read about marriage and divorce facts, the victory of logic over emotions or vice versa would be a matter of personal character. The option of cohabiting before marriage is helpful in restraining the overwhelming sense of infatuation, so that logic might find a chance for evaluating the hard, hidden facts of marital life, nowadays. However, even cohabiting may not help much for many reasons. Partners may become dependent and addicted to each other's love and task-sharing conveniences before they get a chance to express their needs and find a suitable relationship model for them. More importantly, though, people's true characters often emerge only after marriage. People change a lot too, rather unexpectedly, especially when some new adventures or financial incentives lure them. Sadly, modern societies are immensely conducive to corrupting people and their marriages.

Aside from the issue of love—even when we think we are immune to the blinding effects of love, and when we believe we are a logical person—we can still get trapped in a marriage for some other irrational thoughts or beliefs. In particular, we usually trust our logic too much and think, "Why should I go through the hassle of evaluating divorce scenarios and viewing marriage as a romantic business *when I really know and trust my partner* already?"

Knowing Our Partner

Many of this author's writings stress on the task of 'knowing ourselves' to enrich our lives and avoid life's traps. Our ability to understand our needs and ourselves helps our relationships, too. Yet, knowing 'who we are' is a challenging venture, even if we acknowledge a need for it. Those absorbed in their Egos, especially, believe they know who they are very well already, anyway. Realistically, though, it takes a lot of modesty, effort, perseverance, and motivation to learn 'who we are.'

We are supposedly a fair, conscious judge of our actions, emotions, and thoughts, yet remain doubtful forever as to 'who we really are.' We can never penetrate into our unconscious mind enough to fathom the truth about our essence—the 'self,' which holds the secret of 'who we are.' We touch and sense certain traces of it occasionally when some novel dimensions of our being unfold before our eyes unexpectedly, usually through a profound thought or a deep sensation, perhaps love for another person.

We might discover certain things about ourselves and our 'self' gradually if we are patient and persistent. Sometimes, our discovery is enlightening or shocking to us. Still, realizing our identity is a tough, lengthy process, despite our allegedly analytical brains, objectivity, deep convictions and thoughts, and all the controls we believe to have over our behaviour, emotions, judgments, and attitudes. Therefore, finding who we really are remains only an abstract idea for most of us.

Now, if knowing 'who we are' is next to impossible in spite of our relative acquaintance with 'self,' just imagine how hard it would be for any of us to know 'who they are.' How naive we are to think that we know our partner adequately—enough to even marry him/her! This is practically impossible, since even our partner does not know 'who s/he is,' let alone an outsider who surely has no access even to her/his conscious or subconscious.

The situation gets more complicated in close relationships. Not only we think we know who we are and who they are, but also **we assume they (our prospective partners) know 'who they are.'** We assume that the way our partner is presenting her/himself to us is based on his/her knowledge of who s/he is, or at least s/he is honest about his/her presentations of his/her character. In reality, however, our partner is not only unaware of who s/he is, but most likely confused about his/her identity like the rest of us, while showing off a phony personality, too. We assume that all of his/her reactions and judgments are well studied and coordinated according to some logical and valid knowledge of who s/he is, when in reality s/he is drawing on any of his/her three aspects of personality to deal with us at any time, usually with little conscious or conscience.

There are still other erroneous assumptions on our part. Not only we think we know who we are and who they are, and not only we assume that they know who they are and they remain faithful to who they are in dealing with us, **we also assume they know 'who we are.'** How many times have we heard ourselves complain and feel disappointed when we thought that our partner did not know us (after all this time and after everything we have done for him/her)? And still we continue with our poor logic to assume that s/he should have known us and our expectations, since we have tried to explain everything to him/her so many times (god knows through which aspect of our personality). Another major fact is that even if our partner was smart and motivated enough to attempt to know 'who we are,' s/he would not be able to really find out who we are for the same reason we would never know who they are. Others understand us according to their perceptions, which is always a limited point of view. And the matter gets more complicated when all of us try to display fake personalities in order to fit in or get accepted. We try to hide our naiveté and instead become too haughty to assert ourselves and prove our identities. In all, it is too naive to expect people understand us.

The dilemma of knowing 'who we are' and 'who they are' grows a few more levels. For example, we can ponder the case in which we assume our partner believes that we know 'who we are,' etc. Or, we might think that what we do not know about our partner's family background, genes, and growing experiences do not affect the outcome of our relationship. Yet, they often do. Parents and relatives interfere and influence our married lives often as well, either indirectly or directly. All these factors confuse even our partners more every day about 'who they are or should be.'

Ironically, our natural obsession to figure out people (know who they are) is an endless, exhausting, frustrating, and futile effort we cannot give up. It is just a natural human tendency, maybe a biological design, for handling people. And the closer people are to us, and the more we should deal with them, the more we feel pressed to figure them out as best as we can to face them most appropriately, mainly as a defence mechanism, but also for many other purposes.

One main hurdle for knowing ourselves and our partners is that we resort to different aspects of our personalities to gauge, communicate with, and manipulate one another. Very seldom we use our 'self' aspect of personalities in our encounters to remain sincere. If we did, we would have a much better chance to understand and know one another. Instead, we use our Egos and Models often to hide our intentions and secrets, and to satisfy our egoistic needs. Using different aspects of our personality does not only prevent us from knowing who we are and who they are. It also contaminates the contents and meanings of relationships. We pretend to be a nice person to attract someone we think we love or want to lure. We hide our tremendous egoism and selfish desires until the initial love fever subsides. We learn about humans' vulnerability and use this knowledge to manipulate one another as much as we can. For example, we manipulate our partner with our superficial compliments just to boost his/her Ego. The strange thing about human nature is that we welcome these compliments even when we know they are insincere.

In many instances, we block the channels of information subconsciously and inadvertently. For example, when we are in love, we keep justifying our partners' intentions. Our 'love need' is simply too strong to give logic and facts a real chance. We just do not want to lose our companion even if we have to deceive ourselves by closing our minds to the obvious signs of egoism and bad character that radiates from our prospective partner readily. We continue to give a benefit of a doubt to our partner, but at the same time develop a barrel of doubts about who we and our partners are. These doubts do not get resolved as long as we keep justifying our own or our partners' actions and intentions. This accumulation of doubts about our partners and our identities hurt our relationships and psyches. We fight with our rising inner conflicts, while we cannot think straight or accept the risk of losing the person we love.

Without getting into more details for our narrow purpose in this book, it suffices to realize that partners' naïve assumptions about knowing each other is hardly correct, even if they have been in love, maybe even after a long-term relationship. Those naïve assumptions become direct causes for stress and major disappointments. Even more amazing is how we intentionally ignore the obvious signs of personality issues, incompatibility, or even a person's crooked motives when we seemingly fall in love with him/her or feel lonely!

Most amazingly, we also have a gross misperception about our abilities to make someone change to our liking with the power of our love or logic (let alone both)! Long discussions about this topic, expecting change, are offered in Chapter Ten, Pages 159-168.

PART II

Divorce

CHAPTER FIVE
Divorce Decision

The toughest decision, under normal life circumstances, comes about when a marital relationship collapses, especially if young children are involved. Not only the pain of separation and legal hassles, but also deep scars hurt partners and their children for many years. Most divorced individuals agree with this assertion. On the other hand, most married couples gauge their options regularly, while their hardships due to alienation compete with the prospects of separation and divorce agonies. When partners' defects are extensive and obvious, the decision is easier. However, a separation decision often gets difficult, because most people have borderline psychological flaws—which still make them incompatible and wicked—and yet the decision becomes only a matter of partners' tolerance level.

Partners' imperfections, which appear somewhat normal individually, clash in relationships severely. Thus, the degree of their incompatibility and malice grows many folds very fast. At the same time, partners are unable to set their tolerance level realistically, because they have no reliable view of the expected (acceptable) level of conflicts in relationships in the new era. Without enough self-control and wisdom, they let their Egos drive all their decisions, including the matter of a desired tolerance level for a typical marital relationship. In fact, many people are less willing or able, nowadays, to live with the inconveniences of marital life, mainly due to their drive for individuality and a foolish sense of self-importance. Therefore, with the first signs of problem, they look for a way out. Conversely, another group takes plenty of abuse, but are too weak to face the matter in a constructive way. Most of us, however, fall between these two extremes. We have adequate tolerance to accept some of the deficiencies of marital life, but also enough pride to consider the option of separation if things REALLY do not work. This large group usually has the most difficult time in making a decision, though, because not only it is never clear when to give up tolerating and depart, but also the repercussions of separation and divorce feel quite severe to these sensible people. As a result, we, the majority, must live with life and marriage hardships, but also struggle with our incessant doubts about the validity and viability of our painful, confusing relationships and the future of our sad marriages. These doubts are overwhelming and often linger a lifetime.

This social dysfunction has obviously spread since we no longer know how to relate to one another in society. In our marriages, especially, we walk into a trying trap, because most of us do not know enough about relationships' unique needs to make our marriages work. It is a trap, since divorce often feels awkward and depressing, especially when our youth is wasted and there are many opposing factors to consider. **These are the kind of knowledge (point of reference) we should rely on for thinking divorce when contemplating marriage—** before getting trapped in a position where the alternatives to our miserable marriages appear even more depressing.

Separation is the hardest life decision (within a normal life setting), because we often end up in a less favourable position than we like to be (or imagine initially). Opting for divorce hastily or living with the agony of indecision about separation has its own stressful outcome. In either case, we cause pain for ourselves and our kids—when we seek divorce rashly or when we struggle to save our marriage futilely. Going by statistics, too many of us choose the divorce solution, because it seems easier and most appealing to our Egos, too. In this state of mind, we consider divorce the only solution, because we have tolerated enough already. Our false pride has been damaged, in particular. And our sense of individualism, independence, and equality is threatened. However, perhaps we are not there yet and a chance for saving our relationship exists if we stop being hostile and hasty in arriving at such a negative conclusion. Thus, this becomes **the point of reference (the reason) for thinking marriage when separation appears more viable and easier.** Pondering marriage is merely the idea of creating an atmosphere for relaxing our minds to think through things more clearly.

We contemplate marriage in order to revive the mood of romanticism that had started this relationship, which is needed now more than ever. In addition, we think about marriage to pinpoint the issues that have now contaminated a relationship that had seemed so logical initially. What promises and factors had made the strength and roots of this relationship? We want to explore what and how things have changed our relationship and us. We want to see if we would come up with a different solution if we could set our Ego aside a few days. We wish to evaluate the viability of forces that might keep us together to fulfil the *real* purposes of marriage, instead of just focusing on personal whims or fussing over irresolvable human issues. The question to ask is whether it is possible to remarry our partner after we have drifted apart inadvertently due to egoism or ignorance. Have we tried to communicate in a constructive manner to evaluate and resolve our differences and to express our ideas in a logical manner? Have we become so alienated that separation seems to be the only solution? And for those of us who still have a chance to save our relationships, we must know what stirs alienation. Furthermore, we want to know our yardsticks for drawing the borderline between tolerance and divorce. We want to reset our expectations and list the criteria and rules that we consider useful for relating with our partner within a new relationship model in order to save our marriage. We like to consider the chance and conditions for remarrying our existing spouse if starting all over were a viable, sensible option. Could we adopt a different relationship model in order to stay together (somewhat more independently and passively perhaps, if necessary), instead of opting for divorce?

Many divorces could have been avoided if partners had a bit more patience and flexibility and had used their Self rather than letting their Egos guide (deceive) them in such a crucial time. Our wild imaginations deceive us about a more caring and smarter partner waiting out there for us. We allow our false pride and rigidity dictate the decisions of separation and divorce, whereas some compassion and forgiveness could have saved a lot of hassle and misery for both partners and their children. Conversely, we might have gained at least some peace of mind and independence if we had made a decision to separate from our spouse when the relationship had seemed doomed, despite our honest efforts to reconcile our personality differences and marital deficiencies. To reiterate, the principal question partners should ask themselves is whether another relationship model exists for them to adopt for living together (perhaps a bit more independently and passively, if necessary) as a wiser alternative to divorce.

The decision of separation and divorce is quite easy, and least consequential, when both partners believe *sincerely* and objectively that alternatives to their existing marital affair are definitely more promising and separation is to their advantage. A decision under this circumstance is easy if partners are in a sound mental condition to make an honest assessment of their needs. However, it is usually hard to be sincere in our beliefs (mostly about separation), because we do not know how to curb our Egos and fantasies even for a few days to gauge the situation realistically without bias and spite. The decision gets difficult when our Egos take charge of the situation and ruin our objectivity even if we were a logical person. Ego kills our ability for tolerance and reflection. Consequently, partners get engaged in endless pursuit of power struggles and petty shows of individualism (based on their own short-sighted definitions of individualism and independence, of course). And when it is not egoism hindering the communication, partners do not know the mechanism of cooperating to resolve their problems, thus resort to the option of separation.

In some extreme instances, one partner has special personal plans, extramarital affairs, or just makes a unilateral decision about separation without paying any attention to the needs and desires of his/her partner. In these situations, separation would most likely be inevitable and the other partner is doomed to accept an imposed decision. It would be too late to convince the demanding partner to change his/her mind, and the chance for reconciling their differences is often very little. One partner has already made the decision for both of them in such cases.

Pre and Post-Divorce Hardships

Our attempts to make a right decision about divorce cause lots of inner conflict, while we struggle and suffer on an alienation course incessantly. This dire condition is explained in the next chapter. When the decision is to separate, however, a new set of challenges besiege us. We should redefine ourselves as a fully independent person in our heads again and perform a barrage of duties on our own. Especially, the matter of raising kids almost single-handedly would prove to put a big burden on our psyches and other aspects of our lives. We like to find another companion, but the task would become increasingly frustrating and futile. The hassles of the legal process, child custody and sharing routines, financial pressures, and the pains of endless quarrels on many issues with our ex-spouse could ruin our careers, mental state, and many years of our lives.

Indeed, post-divorce hardships are too horrendous and vast to include in this book in detail, but enough clues are made along the way. The emphasis in this book is on pre-divorce issues and hardships, because if we succeed to avoid a divorce we would be avoiding the harsher hardships of post-divorce. The irony is that our misperceptions about marriage objectives and our opportunities after divorce often prevent us, nowadays, to analyse the state of our relationships realistically. We are lured into favouring a divorce decision prematurely. Thus, it is important to learn about the alienation process and debilitating 'separation thoughts' that a majority of couples encounter in their relationships. If we learn about the inevitable hardships of all marriages and divorces, as well as our roles to manage our relationships more effectively, we increase our chances for living a less hectic life and avoiding the big divorce mistake.

Separation Path

Usually a long, rough path leads to separation. From the early days of honeymoon and love, we embark upon a jerky journey in search of intimacy and a friendly relationship. However, like any long journey, the road is full of hazards and turmoil. *Sneaky storms* erupt after we set sail so enthusiastically on this rough journey. Some obscure and adverse currents destroy our enthusiasm and redirect our focus towards a new, ambiguous destination. Our search for intimacy fails and we enter a new phase of relationship, which feels more like an alienation path. Every day we feel more estranged and drifting further apart from our partner until we can hardly see or feel each other. Naturally, everybody abhors this looming destination and the depressing idea of 'separation.' This option had hardly crossed our minds when getting married; or perhaps we had recklessly dismissed the chance to study it. Somehow, however, we have now arrived at this destination unexpectedly. We are shocked and confused, yet the reason for arriving at this point is clear:

Estrangement happens when we lose sight of our initial goal and destination (marriage purposes) and drift away mentally to a point where we cannot see our partner eye to eye; we cannot help each other stir the boat in the same direction. It happens when we do not recognize or work actively on 'Relationships Success Factors.' Thus, we arrive at an odd destination we had not sailed for, and feel lonely, tired, and confused. We have just gotten there since we had drifted away from our original course mostly out of ignorance, stubbornness, and spite.

The long, lonely journey of 'alienation' brings us immense disappointments, disagreements, hurts, turmoil, anxiety, and anger. Soon the time comes when our sweet dreams and love are gone and our relationship enters a bizarre, new phase of constant doubts and evaluation. We assess our marriage, our partner, our expectations, and the prospects of the existing dire arrangement. A deep sense of doubtfulness and an urge to gauge our options overwhelm our minds gradually, as we live in a haze with our pressing life responsibilities and struggles. We question the sensibility of our life and relationship and look for a solution. Our doubts about, and search for, a refuge intensify during marital conflicts or when we withdraw in a state of shock temporarily. Naturally, we are disappointed with the outcome of our married life and build deep cynicism about the value and validity of marriage in general. The more we are disappointed and discouraged regarding our relationship and unfulfilled expectations, and the more cynical we get about our sanity to live in this condition, the more we feel alienated towards our partner. Our initial attraction and trust are readily replaced by doubts, suspicions, and resentment.

If these thoughts and feelings sound familiar, you are most likely on an alienation course and now is time to do something about it fast. Maybe it is actually a very good time to ponder marriage—i.e., remarrying your present spouse after finding a viable relationship model to bear each other's idiosyncrasies better.

The Turmoil

Partners are usually unaware of their marital atmosphere and how poorly they relate to each other. Thus, they do not notice their alienation journey until it is too late to return. They face a big turmoil swiftly. Maybe when we are in the early stages of this journey, we could return to the main road, but not after we have travelled a long distance and fallen apart from our partner completely. We would simply not have enough stamina and motivation to travel back even if we could discover the road to return. At some point and time, eventually the road to return is eroded by severe storms and upheavals. Some of us might be lucky in eluding the alienation journey due to our personalities without even realizing it, but most people are susceptible to embark upon this journey fast when our marital relationships start to deteriorate. If we are nonchalant about the hazards of this journey and unprepared to fight alienation traps actively, we soon find ourselves in a no-return zone only able to move forward where the journey usually ends in turmoil, separation, or perhaps a lifelong of desolation at the very best.

Naturally, alienation is mainly the outcome of unmatched or faulty personalities unnoticed or ignored before marriage. When we discover our partner's shortfalls, and as we realize our naivety in trying to change him/her, we get discouraged and adopt an attitude of resistance or carelessness that leads to more conflicts and misunderstandings. We prefer to withdraw than fight on issues that we finally accept as irresolvable and irreconcilable. Misunderstandings, poor communication skills, and other marital problems also contribute to alienation even if partners had been partially, or even totally, compatible. With our withdrawals, we fuel the process of alienation. In addition, initial respect and attraction fades away after a cohabitation period and learning about each other's idiosyncrasies. Thus, it gets almost impossible to reverse the course of alienation and separation. All that initial love and enthusiasm seem to vanish and one or both partners wonder about the fast turn of events and loss of passion.

Reversing Our Focus

While it is wise to prevent mismatched marriages, our focus should reverse after marriage. That is, the burden of proof resides on partners' shoulders to show why their differences cannot be worked out if their psychological defects and Egos are not drastic and uncontrollable; and if the logic and some flares of love that existed at the time of marriage is still intact. Even unmatched partners might have a chance to reconcile their differences if they remain aware and resist the temptation of going deeply on an alienation journey. Most importantly, they must know about and work proactively on Relationships Success Factors listed in Table 3.1 on page 31.

Another major problem is that we do not recognize the hidden traps in marriage and the ways they lead to alienation. Thus, naively we leave the prospect of our marriage to chance and destiny, because we do not know how to play an active role in recognizing and avoiding alienation entrapments. Most cases of alienation relate to partners' inability to communicate well, although they might be relatively compatible. Actually, even incompatible partners with mutual attraction and ability to communicate succeed better than matched couples who do not learn to communicate. This is unfortunate, since partners trap themselves on the alienation journey unnecessarily and wastefully. Another sizeable portion of separations is due to innocent miscommunications that exhaust partners' patience and level of tolerance.

The alienation process starts with small disappointments. However, these letdowns accumulate quickly when partners do not handle them collectively and promptly. Staying vigilant regarding the destructive power and outcome of alienation, partners can learn to fight the circumstances and personal urges that stir alienation. They can learn about those interactions and delicate situations that cause misunderstandings, hurt feelings, and alienation. They should also realize the repercussions of their sinister attitudes (including hasty judgments about each other, misperceptions, idiosyncrasies, and harsh tone of voice) as alienation causes, conditions, and torments.

We can find all kinds of examples and typical situations that lead to alienation. For one thing, our (changing) image of our partner initiates the process of alienation. Our unfulfilled expectations of marital life and our image of a perfect partner stir big misunderstandings. We compare our partner's attitude with our perception of a perfect mate who can fulfil our needs. We merely focus on our own needs and convenience. When our partner cannot match that image, we become extremely disappointed and angry with him/her. Our inability to curb our Ego, when we face such inconveniences, plays a major role in developing alienation.

The high demands and responsibilities of marriage also create alienation when the concepts of teamwork and sensible commitment are not understood and observed. Partners might still have a chance to build a decent relationship together if other hurdles did not stop them. However, they cannot fulfil the main requirements of a successful marriage, because they are not trained for married life properly. And of course, their inexperience regarding marital needs and circumstances and its communication hurdles make them incapable of making the right judgments and decisions, in particular in their first marriage. Usually our second and third marriages—if we ever dare to marry again—have a lesser chance of failure. Is this because we learn a few lessons from our first marriage about the intricacies of relationships and alienation entrapments? Or, we simply give up and decide to be more patient and tolerant, perhaps because we are getting older and feel vulnerable? Or, because we have become wiser and realized that marriage can never be even slightly perfect the way we like it to be? Or, because we are now more careful and knowledgeable about our selection of a companion? Perhaps a combination of all these factors. Yet, many of these lessons could be learned in advance and practised in the first marriage, too, if we merely invest some time and patience. It is just a matter of pondering our marriage and divorce decisions more seriously—possibly in the reverse order if we can!

The Effect of Global Mentality

We usually use a collection of simple examples to arrive at general interpretations. Now let us do the opposite: Infer about marital conflicts by gauging some examples of global mindset. They reflect the generality of social mayhem and its impact on family mentalities. We cannot ignore the widespread problems of nations fighting for independence and self-determination. Religious crusades, ethnic struggles for separation from their motherlands, the Middle East rising chaos, and the Palestine's struggles to get back what Israel has captured as its own with the support of some hypocrite superpowers, are all reflections of who we are as human beings. They demonstrate our general attitudes toward others, which reveal our deep convictions and egoistic view of 'us versus them.' The attitude that 'I know everything, I am the best, but the rest are evil' is the rule of our planet; a fact we nurture and believe in so strongly. We always think we deserve more than the rest. Therefore, we draw a line to signify our borders, to isolate others and to keep everything for ourselves even if what we have is something we borrowed or captured by force from somebody else. It is ours now. It is hard not to wonder regarding some Quebecer's incentive for sovereignty and independence from Canada considering the rather civil existence in Canada for all its residents. An image and dream of being *distinct* from the rest of Canada probably gives them the incentive and stamina to fight for separation. Thus, what is behind this need for 'distinction' that drives us blindly and forcefully regarding this idea and the feelings of alienation? Has our disappointments from human encounters and relationships brought us to such a controversial position? Is it our inner urges pushing us so hard to prove our abilities to be independent? Or, is it just our egoism to prove our being in the most retaliatory and controversial way? These very same urges and forces that drive and convolute our social thinking and patriotic struggles prevail in our personal lives as well. In fact, they both are derived from the same source—the egoism dictating our personal beliefs and needs. The malicious forces and egos that define and run our work habits and organizations dominate our marriages as well.

Our selfish needs are reinforced by prevalent social values and 'generally-practised' attitudes and expectations of other fellow humans. We reinforce each other's Ego to strive for foolish and unnecessary means of building and expressing our individualism, identity, and importance. The dire alienation process in marital life is mainly influenced by these very same fundamentals of human nature and demented ways of modern thinking.

We get married with false expectations that are bound to fail, anyway. We burden our marital relationships by so many demands and a haughty display of individualism, as if carrying the torch of separation from day one in our heads without even realizing it. Even marriage itself is often considered only an exercise for separation from bachelorhood, which we feel is constricting our identity as someone who can (and must) be loved and needed. We think of marriage as a venue to portray our individualism. We ignore that marriage is not a platform for expression of individualism and personal Ego or satisfying our personal needs. This mentality actually defeats the notion of developing personal independence. 'Individualism' requires humility and selflessness. Unfortunately, however, in society and marital life we interpret 'individualism' in a wrong way as a means of showing off our Egos and expressing personal power and abilities, whereas in fact the emphasis should be placed on humility, teamwork, and objectivity. Ironically, our obsession for a companion and marriage is mostly a sign of our inability or unwillingness to be an independent individual! Most of us are too needy and soft to exercise independence or understand the true meaning of individualism. However, we insincere humans do not stop pretending otherwise, anyway.

Our initial, exaggerated expectations of marriage create the basic hurdles in building our relationships properly. Our first thoughts in marriage are about those things that we expect from our partners and all the great things that should now start happening. We are unaware of marriage requirements and all the new things that we should do for our relationships and partners. We have no vision of the demands on us to cope with the new way of life. We do not realize the sacrifices that are needed to stabilize our relationships and how our personal Egos should be managed more tightly to do that. We do not know or think about the responsibilities we must carry in a relationship and the delicate role we must play. Therefore, we do everything the wrong way by expressing a false personality in the hope of asserting our individuality and dominating the situation. Only when we learn the implications of an alienation journey, how it starts, and what triggers it, we may learn about the damaging roles we play in instigating alienation. We play a forbidding role when our attitudes and values alienate our partners. And we play another negative role when our partners alienate us and we just resort to retaliation, instead of dealing with the situation calmly and effectively.

Fortunately, an opposite path to alienation is available for sincere, smart couples to elude the high chances of alienation and separation, but also flourish their marriages to an enviable stance. We could envision and follow this sacred path merely by staying alert about 'marriage purposes' and 'relationships success factors' suggested in this book. Instead of allowing our naiveté and high expectations mislead us on an alienation journey early in our marriages, we could follow an 'Alienation awareness path,' as discussed in Chapter Seven, and remain objective and active about marriages' realistic purposes and means of accomplishing them. First, it is helpful to understand alienation characteristics and preparedness, which are reviewed in the next two chapters.

CHAPTER SIX
Alienation Characteristics

Since alienation is the main road to separation, it helps to realize its characteristics and prevent it from infecting our relationships—before it becomes too late. We can beware of the symptoms of alienation that creeps up in our marriage slowly and destroys the relationship eventually.

Alienation is a *feeling* of dissociation with our partner and his/her ideas. It is a feeling of loss of influence on the direction of our relationship, and a lack of strength and motivation to do anything about it. We see our partner in a different light all of a sudden. Our new image of our partner is quite unfamiliar and causes internal unrest when we think about him/her. We feel estranged, as though we do not know him/her. We do not understand her/his logic and reasoning when analysing the facts of life and our marriage. No common ground exists for discussing our interests and needs, we do not trust his/her judgment, we feel falling more adrift from him/her every day, and we become more doubtful regarding our relationship. The level of intimacy appears to decline along with our respect for him/her, and we feel strange and uncomfortable in his/her presence.

In addition, alienation is a *state of mind* in which we give up arguing about issues and changes that we sought from our partner before. We prefer to stay passive and keep a distance from our partner in order to eliminate or reduce conflicts and arguments. We quit reasoning and often surrender to whims and desires of our partners, not because we agree with them, but rather because we doubt if our viewpoints have any value or effect for restoring our relationship. We feel emotionally defeated and exhausted by even the thought of approaching our partner to discuss or ask for something. We fear him/her and resent arguments may erupt at any point and any time we are together. We fear the games, intimidations, blaming, and nagging that usually erupt when we are together. Our contacts are unpleasant, thus we try to minimize and control them. If we lack enough inner strengths and a healthy self-image, we might eventually feel miserable with loss of control of our life on top of the relationship itself.

Milder alienation trips start in our marriage before we get to the real alienation journey. We all walk on and off the alienation path anytime we feel desolation or disappointment with our partners. The severity of conflicts rises only when we advance further out on this journey. Otherwise, mostly subtle and mild alienation trips set us off during our superficial and innocent arguments. Then, we usually return to the main path of togetherness and cooperation. Yet, while the effects of these alienation trips may be much less critical, so many trips—however short they may be—would eventually exhaust us and contaminate our relationship. Frequent trips eventually set off the big journey of alienation.

Partners' depression naturally affects their sense of physical attraction and enjoyment. They engage in sexual relationships for lust rather than a feeling of love. John Gray's analogy of 'men going to their caves' in his book[†] is a reference to this alienation process. However, it appears that both genders are equally moody rather regularly, and thus withdraw from their

---

[†] *Men are from Mars, Women are from Venus,* Harpercollins; Harperperennial, 1992.

partners emotionally and physically on a cyclical routine. On some occasions, in fact, women show a higher tendency for withdrawal, especially during menstruation. The mood cycles are, nonetheless, reinforced when partners are on an alienation course, however mild or subtle the alienation may be. Overall, men do not appear to 'go to their caves' more frequently than women do, considering the latter's natural urges and the effect of their hormones. Actually, it happens more to women also due to their higher emotional personality, for sensing and proving a higher need for autonomy these days, or perhaps for being from the planet Venus with a very peculiar mindset. In all, women are often more sensitive and demanding, and thus show a higher tendency to withdraw. A significant difference exists in the nature of withdrawals between men and women, though. Men's withdrawal is usually passive, as they just hide in their shells. Women's, on the other hand, is usually showy, retaliatory, and spiteful. It might sound odd, however, to stress that women's withdrawal could actually appear rather sneaky or diplomatic as well.

Several factors, including lower Model and higher Ego, make men more abrupt in their withdrawal, when their sense of alienation reaches its height temporarily. That is, when one partner goes on an alienation journey, perhaps even without realizing it, both partners would be inclined to keep a distance and avoid unnecessary contacts that would cause arguments. However, gradually the force of sexual needs begins to take over. At this stage, either men or women begin to crawl out of the cave and approach their partners for the eventual goal of satisfying their lust. Since men are usually more aggressive (but more needy and vulnerable) regarding their sexual urges, their emergence from cave is more apparent, thus for the same reason their withdrawal might also appear more transparent and crude. In all, the intensity of alienation sends both genders to their caves according to their prominent personality aspects, and often their high urge for sex brings them out of seclusion.

Being from the planets Venus and Mars, we would expect men and women see each other as aliens at first sight! Thus, the fact that they initially meet naturally and peacefully, fall in love, and express their intimacy and feelings toward each other easily is puzzling and contradictory. This is how and why it is hard to fathom the sources of subsequent problems. If men and women are good and nice to each other initially, with no sense of being aliens, then something bizarre makes them see each other's real personalities after marriage so differently, in a way that had not been obvious before, or at least had not felt so unbearable. Only partners' new perceptions, after marriage, stir their views of each other as aliens, if not mean enemies. Therefore, it appears that men and women are from the planet Earth, after all, as they set out so naturally to get married and make all kinds of woes and commitments to one another. However, everybody has a unique perspective and priorities in life, which also change regularly. Surely, people vary in terms of their visions and aspirations. When these differences are not recognized as inherent aspects of human nature, and when we insist on complete equality and uniformity (including partners' intelligence level), we get into trouble due to our new, naïve expectations from marriage. Furthermore, when marriages are not bound by sensible guidelines and commitments, they fall into alienation traps quickly and easily due to our varied, vain perceptions of marriage.

In all, it appears that mainly alienation makes partners see each other as aliens from outer space and unable to relate even when they try to explain or listen to each other. Sometimes, we think that our partner is resisting the opportunity to learn and is deliberately fighting our thoughts, suggestions, and ideas about cooperation.

We might eventually get fed up with our marriage and think that time has come to separate. Before we reach this final point, we are usually aware of the process and long period of alienation. Yet, we often are not consciously aware of how we are travelling on this alienation path, and then suddenly reach the end of the road and feel fed up. Or, we continue to live in a state of alienation for the rest of our lives without ever making the final decision to separate. The decision is hard, because we usually do not know where we stand in our relationships and cannot gather enough evidences from all the signs that erupt regularly on the alienation road. We are besieged by huge doubts about our conclusions, relationship, and existence as a whole, and do not know how to deal with them.

Alienation Process

During an initial grace period after marriage, partners try to adjust to the new environment, routines, and expectations, and at the same time express (and assert) their views of marital life and plans. Partners test each other and try to prove themselves. They cleverly gauge their positions in their relationship and play all aspects of their personalities to adapt, accommodate, express love, but, most of all, mark their territories. Often a lot of passion and compassion is exchanged as partners share common interests to raise their life enjoyments. The freshness of the experience lets partners forget their other engagements and obligations temporarily to emphasize on the activities and conversations around their new joint mission. Optimism and cooperation prevail and future looks bright and filled with promises. Oh, how much we all miss that sweet period!

Soon, however, the reality kicks in and partners remember the importance of their other activities and responsibilities. They go back to their old habits and activities gradually, and accept marital life as a new foundation for accommodating all other activities and life objectives. Real life issues feel vivid and serious again, thus our level of attention to our partner and his/her interests stabilize at a level that is convenient for us; not the level that our partner expects in his/her sensitive mind.

Strangely enough, while we balance our activities and level of attention to our partner's needs according to our needs and sense of practicality, we continue to expect our partner to give us the same high level of love and attention that we need and had imagined prior to marriage. We perceive our balancing act a practical move, but conceive our partner's adjustment a loss of his/her interest, thus a threat to our relationship. We start to doubt our partner's intentions, love, and commitment. And we cultivate the first seeds of mistrust and alienation. Alienation is not quite serious at this point, but it deteriorates fast, unless partners learn to reconcile their mentalities and activities with the generic relationship requirements in the new era.

Accordingly, partners are baffled by both their own cooling down and their spouse's adjusted attitude. The change and the confusion then lead to hurt feelings and reactions, openly or indirectly. Perhaps some hints and casual discussions of hurt feelings surface occasionally, each partner trying to justify his/her own intentions, but criticizing his/her partner's cooling attitude. Partners' hidden flaws and anxiety start to erupt in the form of insecurities, possessiveness, jealousy, withdrawals, etc., especially for couples who have relied too much on love to carry their relationships. Egos are usually under attack and partners' frustrations explode in different ways. Their reactions set the pace for the next level of struggles. Hostile discussions and never-ending futile arguments make their lives miserable. Those who are less tolerant, or perhaps more practical in their minds, might give up already and consider separation at this stage. However, the majority of us continue with our fights, withdrawals, and doubts, with hopes that someday our partner would understand our needs and demands and stop resisting our request to change.

We do not recognize that change is impossible even if our partner had all the best intentions to change. Nevertheless, the conditions continue to deteriorate, since we do not know how to handle the situation and soothe our injured Egos. We start to doubt the value of our arguments and the possibility of our partner ever caring for us enough to change, although we keep pushing him/her in different ways, anyhow. Especially, if a mutual attraction exists, we continue to go through a cycle of arguments and fights - hostility and withdrawal - make up and sex - logical confrontation and justification - back to the start of the cycle—a new round of ferocious fights. However, every time we go through this cycle, a little bit of intimacy is scraped off our relationship. We lose confidence about our relationship and wonder if our arguments would ever lead to any tangible results. We feel more alienated towards our partner and less interested to discuss the contentious issues. We start to doubt our decision to marry this odd person. Unfortunately, we find that the number of issues we avoid discussing rises gradually until there is really not much left to say to each other outside the very essentials, in a hostile tone.

However, we still do not wish to give up. We are alienated somewhat, maybe a lot even. However, underneath all those doubts about the viability of our marriage and the fruitfulness of our struggles, some glimpses of optimism and hope keep us going. Both partners carry the burdens of alienation and the heaviness of their silence, but neither dares or cares to initiate a conversation that would eventually instigate more fights and disappointments. Partners feel helpless alongside their doubts and despair, but alternatives do not appear promising, either. Thus, no attempt is made to do anything with the relationship but to tolerate it, for now at least.

The alienation grows gradually even through unintentional rudeness, misunderstandings, and insensitive comments. Often, partners' idiosyncrasies expedite the alienation, usually in an early stage of marriage and proceeds hastily towards its final destination, as if they were travelling on a supersonic airplane rather than a sailboat. Surely, partners' personalities, especially their patience, affect the process and speed of alienation a lot. Yet, the outcome and eventuality of separation do not change much if a couples' alienation reaches a point where return feels insurmountable. Therefore, if partners' personalities are vastly different and cannot find some means of cooperation to elude alienation, they are better off following the speedy process of ending everything quickly with minimal bloodshed. Long alienation journeys are suffocating and excruciating.

Innocent Causes of Alienation

Even minor personal idiosyncrasies and miscommunications cause alienation. A simple and subtle communication might be misunderstood and reacted upon antagonistically. Partners often raise old issues in hopes of clarifying a particular point or resolving an outstanding issue. Yet, this seemingly logical attempt makes them anxious, especially when the main topic of discussion vanishes in the midst of quarrels. For example, (A) innocently raises a particular old incident to demonstrate a general idea or a weakness in their relationship. However, (B) uses the occasion to argue about the relevance of the example and (A)'s hidden intentions to raise it again now. By itself, (A)'s example is merely meant to signify an event in the past, a life experience that might have some educational value. Yet, since (A) has brought up an old event, the argument is swiftly redirected towards a deeper marital problem. (A) is blamed again for insensitivity, and s/he is dragged into a faultfinding exercise that leads only to more futile arguments.

In the early stages of marriage, especially, partners do not even fathom the causes of their outbursts from simple ideas or observations, except that they get into lengthy arguments over issues that did not matter anymore. They end up sleeping in different rooms and do not talk for perhaps a week or two with no real reason to support such childish behaviours. They might get smarter eventually and analyse their conversations through reflection and find the causes of their conflicts and arguments. They might realize how they let their spouses drag them into useless arguments based on simple conversations or opinions with no direct relevance to, or importance for, their marriage. Eventually, partners may learn to avoid raising points that trigger faultfinding arguments about past events, which means they never give themselves a chance to learn anything from their experiences. The funny thing is that when a partner talks about a new issue, the other partner interrupts him/her often and asks, "Like what? Give me an example." (However, they both know better now that raising contentious experiences only open the can of worms all over again for a new round of arguments.)

Understanding simple conditions that trigger arguments and fights in marriage (such as the example noted above) does not mean that we can always avoid such explosive situations. Rather, this knowledge might raise our awareness of normal conditions that often lead to miscommunication. The causes of miscommunications are numerous and unique for each couple. They, however, can make an effort to pinpoint those special topics or situations that trigger miscommunication. Strangely enough, often the causes of miscommunication are simple and mostly irrelevant to the issue at hand. They usually reflect the hidden problems and neglected needs of one or both partners, awaiting an opportunity to erupt indirectly in a middle of daily conversation. If not, it relates to the poor way each person handles the process of communication and how information is received, analysed, and reacted to. John Gray's book refers to simple examples of miscommunication. Some of his examples are:

"Women say: 'We never go out,'

men hear: 'You are not doing your job. What a disappointment you have turned out to be ..., you are lazy, unromantic, and just boring.,'

they mean: 'I feel like going out and doing something together.'" Ibid., page 62.

"Women say: 'Everyone ignores me,'
men hear: 'I am so unhappy, I just can't get the attention I need. Everything is completely hopeless. You should be ashamed. You are unloving.,'
they mean: 'Today, I am feeling ignored and unacknowledged. Would you give me a hug and tell me how special I am to you?'" Ibid., page 63.

"Men say: 'I'm fine,' and
women hear: 'I don't care about what has happened. This problem is not important to me. Even if it upsets you, I don't care.,'
They mean: 'I am fine because I am successfully dealing with my upset or problem. I don't need any help. If I do I will ask.'" Ibid., page 74.

These interpretations are not necessarily complete or true as a rule, but they reflect how our miscommunications trigger our senses of insecurity and oversensitivity. Some interesting conclusions can, however, be deduced from these kinds of (mis)communications. First, they indicate that we hide our real needs and meanings in the context or tone of communications. Second, we expect our partner to be sensitive and intelligent enough to understand and interpret our meanings from all the miscommunications, moody attitudes, and hidden messages in our conversations. Third, we have become accustomed to this kind of incomprehensive communications and believe it is all right. Fourth, it suggests the necessity of developing a sixth sense for interpreting deliberately ambiguous communications and people should be blamed if their brains cannot learn to do so all the time. We have gotten too selfish to recognize and admit that miscommunication occurs because we express it in a strange and irrelevant manner, or because we have become oversensitive, too demanding, or use a bad tone of voice. Once we start this game (miscommunication filled with futile hints and hidden expectations) between a couple, it becomes a norm and normal routine for both partners to torture each other with their sarcastic, enigmatic communications.

Miscommunication occurs deliberately or innocently for many reasons. In particular, with the increase in individuals' stress level, preoccupation with a variety of problems and tasks, including personal and business priorities, the amount of time and patience necessary for communication never seems enough. We are constantly in a rush to go somewhere else and do something else, and we expect our partner to know this. We expect our partners to not only understand our meaning in a communication even when it is not expressed straight, but also adjust his/her needs and communication style to accept and accommodate this inordinate behaviour. The problem is that the more partners strive to accommodate these infantile expectations, the more convoluted the communication norms become, and the more the chances of miscommunication and alienation get. We never seem interested in solving the sources of problems, but only deal with their symptoms *superficially*. These perfunctory solutions only create more confusion and stress, not to mention all the extra efforts that people must put into even their simple communications.

Couples feel alienated towards each other for unintended and innocent gestures that get out of hand. We hurt each other with our passive/aggressive attitude and communication. We forget that our idiosyncrasies are responsible for causing many miscommunications and alienating situations often without our intention. Non-psychological and external causes of alienation also exist, like financial hardship, social norms, health issues, etc. However, most alienation problems are created because we are not aware and in control of our small flaws, including our persistence to use vague messages and sarcastic tone in our communications. Common causes of alienation among couples are listed below:

Common Causes of Alienation

- Inability to communicate
- Miscommunication, intentional or due to carelessness
- Nagging and blaming
- Hostile or irritable tone of voice during communication
- Reluctance or inability to share information and cooperate
- Lack of trust or respect
- Deceit and insincerity
- Egoism and intimidation
- Lack of passion and compassion
- Personality clashes and incompatibility
- Insecurities and deprivation of personal needs
- Financial or social burdens, and other external factors
- Unbalanced and unsatisfied expectations
- Perception of some or all of the above, especially the lack of love, Etc.

Learning about the alienation process and its causes is crucial for detecting and acknowledging both our personal and marital issues before it is too late. This awareness can help us view marital *relationships* more consciously as a dynamic setting highly susceptible to (mostly self-induced) alienation factors (as listed above). Nonetheless, we are personally responsible for letting these forces interfere and shape our mentalities and relationships. Self-awareness helps us recognize the causes of alienation, adjust our attitudes and expectations, and curb our debilitating habits that promote alienation.

Fighting Alienation

Normally, nobody imagines leaving his/her spouse when s/he is just getting married. We all *imagine* nothing but a smooth and fruitful relationship developing gradually into a thriving, happy partnership. This innocent assumption demonstrates how things often go wrong despite our good intentions. Of course, occasionally a partner changes his/her mind about marriage, thus actively causes alienation to get out of this commitment. When a partner decides to separate, no one and no advice can help the situation and partners.

However, alienation usually starts inadvertently against our good intentions. We prefer to stay married if external forces and partners' inherent quirks would allow it. Yet, always many things go wrong and alienation begins very early on in most marriages, nowadays. Many individuals acknowledge losing their marriage to their own sense of insecurity, which is only one common example of genetic deficiencies partners bring to their marital life and cause endless conflicts. Therefore, we can search seriously for factors, mostly personal defects, that lead to our alienation after marriage.

Alienation is mainly a symptom of some real or perceived outside threat (mainly our spouse) instigating many of our psychological flaws, which we do not know about or cannot control. Usually, an external stimulus, such as our partner's flirting with someone else, provokes our dormant quirks. It triggers our sense of jealousy and insecurity beyond control. In many situations, the external stimulus may not be even real. Rather, only our (mis)perception of external events usually triggers our quirks. Our imagination can drive us crazy if we let it. And, of course, in many cases we become the subject of abuse by our partner without any fault or provocation on our side. We simply receive different kinds of abuse, perhaps even without our partner's direct intention to hurt or alienate us. Conversely, we act in a way (intentionally or inadvertently) that sometimes provokes our partner. In this case, our action becomes an external stimulus for our partner whose reaction we observe and respond to (again) with another rude reaction of our own. Naturally, this series of actions-reactions can lead to further misperceptions, retaliatory exchanges, and of course alienation.

If partners are REALLY serious and sincere about keeping their relationship, and only if they are not extremely flawed beyond repair, they may be able to search for, and find ways of preventing, the causes of alienation. Often, they can take preventative measures against alienation process, although it is a tough task. Mainly, they must become much better persons than they have been to, i) recognize and stop their alienating behaviours, and, ii) tolerate some hardship and psychological insecurities that persist in all relationships. At the same time, by merely expressing or intending to be a 'good' and 'patient' person, we do not actually turn into one over night. It would take many years of conviction and faith to develop and apply these qualities slowly, as explained in the next section.

Acknowledgment and Awareness

The first step to stop alienation is to become a more conscious and conscience person with higher patience and compassion. This mainly means acknowledging our personal shortfalls and realizing their destructive role in causing alienation. We must learn about our personal and relationship needs that often do not coincide, thus create conflicts. We must grasp the roots of our idiosyncrasies and raw mindsets as well as the underlying problems of our unique relationship without getting into deep analysis and drawing conclusions right away. We are simply looking for the main clues regarding the causes of our clashes and conflicts to draw a general picture about the health of our relationship and our crude attitude that causes alienation. This self-assessment, fact-finding process demands total sincerity, commitment, and objectivity. It requires staying clear from criticism and fast conclusions.

When we first look for relationship problems, we are not compelled to acquire our partner's participation or consent. We do not have to ask our partner to sit with us, argue, blame each other, get our Egos worked up, and accomplish nothing at the end. Rather, problem diagnosis is merely a personal awareness exercise. We do everything alone, at least initially, without the involvement of our partner. For example, if we have lost our interest or love in a relationship, we should admit it honestly, instead of looking for excuses as to 'why I have lost my love or respect for him/her.' The reasons are only important at the next stage, only if the possibility of regaining our love and respect for him/her exists. We do not even have to admit our faults or loss of interest to our partner if we do not want to, but at least we should become aware of our own erratic emotions, and eventually start working on them.

We might think that we know all the factors contributing to alienation and we are aware of the process and the rest of it. Yet, this fundamental superficiality and our ignorance about the meaning of awareness make us flop. In addition, we often *think* that only our partner's resistance to listen, ignorance, and other deep defects cause the problems, anyway, while we are extremely conscientious about, and proactive in resolving, our marital problems. We might even believe that our awareness efforts and practising certain roles to prevent alienation are simply a waste of our time, or at least not fair, because we are doing all the work and showing interest to save our marriage while our partner appears more careless every day.

While we can aim for the awareness of both partners and their influence on each other to prevent alienation, we can be only in control of our own awareness process and progress. We are responsible for playing our role consciously without being disturbed or discouraged by our partner's apathy. Our awareness means that we accept our partner's resistance and deal with the possibility of negative attitude and psychological defects of our partner, which may directly interfere and hinder our attempts to spawn awareness in our marital relationship. We must keep playing our role.

Boosting our consciousness and awareness requires deep reflections to become a somewhat selfless and compassionate person slowly. We concentrate on the alienation process itself, rather than our partner's faults, and we play a proactive role to prevent our marriage breakdown, if possible. We avoid using awareness as another level of scrutiny on our partner's lack of understanding and goodwill. Otherwise, we would not grasp the meaning and purpose of awareness. We would only keep blaming our partner and sink deeper in depression and our egoistic personality. That kind of crude approach to awareness would only create more alienation and friction than help. In these circumstances, we also get frustrated and give up quickly when we face our partner's retaliatory actions and spite. Our insincerity and egoism would only confuse us and alienate our partner further as well. Overall, the objective of boosting our consciousness and awareness is to turn inwardly to detect our own flaws and build our strength to fight alienation. Then, we can study those relationship hurdles that often reflect partners' incompatibilities and lower their communication abilities.

One essential fact to remember is that, in most cases, we must prevent alienation on our own. Like all other types of awareness and enlightenment experiences, marital awareness is also a personal mission we pursue mostly for our benefit. It would prove to be a productive way of calming ourselves and reducing the stress caused by the unknown sources of marital conflicts and quarrels. More importantly, however, marital awareness is a personal objective since, in the final analysis, the information and wisdom we develop in the process is for soothing our nerves and preventing a lifelong quarrel with our doubts about the nature and prospect of our relationship. The idea is to gather enough evidence and confidence to make an objective decision about our relationship and future. We must cooperate with our partner and show interest in pursuing a joint awareness process as much and long as possible, but then we would be responsible for our decision, especially if it must be 'separation.'

When we speak to our partner from an awareness platform, s/he might not necessarily grasp or agree with, our views and approach for solving our problems. We should build common grounds for awareness-oriented communication, but only after our primary self-awareness feels genuine and useful. Often we think we are aware of the situation and problems when in fact we are only focusing on our partner's faults and blaming him/her for everything. In such cases, our awareness is not honest and objective, but rather a faultfinding exercise. Our tenacity to convince our partner about relationship issues, and blaming her/him, merely shows our egotism and self-cleansing failure so far. Sadly, however, focusing on each other's faults is the most common approach partners pursue naively. After all, this is the easiest way of copping out, instead of learning, mainly through self-awareness, to cope with relationships' sad realities in the new era. We refuse to acknowledge our share of flaws and responsibilities in causing conflicts, and yet believe we are playing an active role to prevent alienation. We have not yet learned that plenty of tolerance is required, nowadays, to keep a relationship and enjoy its potential benefits.

The bottomline is that we undertake an awareness exercise since we sincerely care about our relationships and lives. That is a significant motive and target. The goal is to help ourselves by remaining objective to identify the real problems and set the course of our lives in a proper direction. We should admit that awareness is more about finding our own faults and share of misunderstandings. It is mostly a process of bringing our Egos in check. And it is more a search for our inner strengths to enhance our self-awareness and communications with our partners. This is the main, and often even the only, objective of self-awareness. Only later, we try to find other sources and external factors that also contribute to alienation. At this stage, we only try to learn about (become aware of) the roots of the problems and our role in creating them. To the extent we can work on the problems unilaterally, we might initiate plans and programs to improve our attitudes and approaches. And to the extent we need to address other issues, including our partner's attitude or perceptions at least, we cannot demand them right away. Rather, we should first establish a mutual understanding with our partner, draw a sensible plan together, and find ways of implementing them together through sincere teamwork.

Ultimately, we must choose the path of our lives with utter wisdom and sincerity. That is the only way we can survive in society and our relationships all in hopes of leading a more purposeful and peaceful existence. That is the ultimate goal of self-awareness as well.

CHAPTER SEVEN
Alienation Preparedness

In all, the purpose of the 'alienation preparedness' process is to monitor and mitigate the rotting relationship conditions that paralyse partners' lives and judgment, as they stagger and struggle on a dismal alienation path. It is just a precautionary antidote for marriage breakdown if a chance to save it exists. It is a preventative measure—vaccine—even if partners have already drifted on the alienation path to some extent. Overall, with alienation preparedness, we plan to maintain the health of our relationships by:

1. Acknowledging potential (general) relationship problems (as well as specific issues in any relationship)
2. Dealing with our psychological defects
3. Measuring and improving our tolerance
4. Recognizing our opportunities and fears
5. Admitting, planning, and playing our roles
6. Making objective judgments and decisions

Partners' perpetual attention to these six steps, as personal responsibilities in relationships, is very important, thus briefly discussed in this chapter. Actually, when reading this book, especially this chapter, ask yourself whether you have enough patience and interest to ponder and care sincerely about the alienation hazards discussed here. Otherwise, the chances of alienation and failure are high for your relationship. Although your partner's participation in the process would be useful, the alienation preparedness factors should be mastered personally first, with the intention and hopes of including your partner in this learning process soon. Surely, it is vital that your partner also has enough sense and interest to join you eventually once you explain the purpose and merits of alienation preparedness process to her/him. Still, you should prepare yourself for this ideal never happening, i.e., your partner's full participation.

Alienation Preparedness - Factor (Goal) One

Acknowledging Potential Relationship Problems

Sadly, we can no longer take our marriages as a *stable* support system (platform) for performing our more tangible life duties. Most of our perceptions of marriage, especially regarding its stability and partners' commitments, are flawed, nowadays. We do not realize that marriage is an ongoing chore and challenge for fulfilling special purposes, while partners should also play specific roles properly and perpetually. Now, marital stability needs constant control and engagement. Even then, marriages remain quite vulnerable forever as a symptom of rising social disorder and people's growing obsession for independence and identity. Sadly, relationships' stability was a luxury that past generations enjoyed so casually, but no more.

Similar to an earthquake, we cannot anticipate the eruption of marriages' fatal turmoil. We can never foresee when one or both partners reach the end of their alienation journey rather unexpectedly and their marriage tumbles under the pressures of alienation, as if a big earthquake had shaken the foundation of their marriage. And similar to an earthquake preparedness program (to foresee and prepare for its severe repercussions), the 'alienation preparedness,' is merely a general plan to boost our awareness about alienation and learn how best to get ready to face it; to at least minimize its effects on ourselves and our families. Some general plans and guidelines are drawn in this chapter, but every person and couple can prepare his/her astute and customized alienation preparedness plan the best in line with partners' personalities and their marriage's peculiarities.

The first step is to study the current marital environment, relationships' unique needs, and circumstances that often lead to alienation. After gaining this general insight, grasping our own and our partners' unique needs and personalities is vital. Most of us take our marriages for granted after a short period of honeymoon, after our passion settles and we touch life's realities again. This does not necessarily mean that we lose our love or enthusiasm that fast. In fact, we often feel secure and comfortable in our marriage, which gives us the psychological safety and a platform to ensue our main life aspirations more actively. This is in line with Maslow's theory that speculates we move on to search and satisfy our higher needs once our lower needs (e.g., belonging and love) are satisfied. Yet, the problem is that we assume our marriage is as safe as we feel about our love and belonging needs. This might not be true. Actually, we often have a wrong perception of marriage at the outset, as we assume that a normal (average) marriage would be safe and manageable, despite all the stories and statistics that suggest otherwise. We assume marital problems emerge only from those exceptional circumstances where partners are not normal or cannot handle their marital affairs logically. Thus, we see no reason to worry, because we consider both ourselves and our marital conditions *normal*. The flaw with these naïve assumptions is that even a 'normal' marriage gets entangled and tainted quickly these days because of the overall malfunctioning of social systems and partners' stress levels, misperceptions, and untamed expectations. Now, no 'normal relationship' exists in society anymore. Thus, we should study and keep three categories of information regarding our marital relationships in mind all the time:

i) Partners' compatibilities and quirks.
ii) Marital environment, with the objective of learning about relationships' specific needs in conjunction with our unique relationship's peculiarities. We must learn about different types of relationship models as well and determine which model best suits partners' personalities and needs.
iii) Main alienating factors in marriage and how to avoid them.

The above three crucial topics have been discussed throughout this book, but especially emphasized in Chapter Eleven.

Alienation Preparedness - Factor (Goal) Two

Acknowledging Our Psychological Defects

After recognizing the sources and severity of our relationship problems, the next step is to acknowledge our idiosyncrasies, as they often taint our relationships. The main goal is to admit that all humans are loaded with defects, and then deal with our own psychological flaws. Our imaginary standards of morality and intelligence vastly surpass average humans' capacity and nature. We imagine ethics and logic much better than we can ever attain as a human. Only when we accept that nobody is even half-perfect as our Egos suggest, or our Models pretend, we might gain the wisdom to better ourselves as a person and a companion, exude more compassion, and prevent alienation.

Therefore, as a basic guideline for civilization, we should follow a rigid self-awareness process, as noted in the previous chapter, to fathom our defects, grasp who we are, and measure the personality that portrays us to others. We learn that our psychological defects are mostly not created or controlled by us. Thus, acknowledging them is not meant to cause shame and guilt in our minds. On the contrary, merely our persistence to ignore them shows our naivety and arrogance. We must be only ashamed of, and feel guilty about, our stubbornness, and our inabilities, to accept the universality and depth of human imperfections. We humans still have a hard time grasping the essence of our being—both our dire impurity and nothingness.

Through soul-searching and self-assessing, we may finally grasp the depth of our psychological defects, and then decide to what extent we wish to control them or let them control us. We need enough maturity to measure these defects and their impacts on our own and other people's lives. We always resist criticism and change, as we think we are perfect already, and that we know everything about ourselves and everybody else. This psychological barrier hinders our search for wisdom and peace. Our addictions to our false personalities and lifestyles stop us from becoming a more natural, purer person, which we believe we can never be, nor see any reason to be. It is like expecting a chronic smoker give up smoking just because he knows the hazards of his habit. Perhaps assuming that we are not aiming to change ourselves, at least not initially, relieves our natural resistance to discover the finer aspects of 'self' and who we really are. Self-cleansing does not create an automatic commitment for change, although our new knowledge of self might lead to a gradual transformation from within without too much effort to bring change about.

We must pinpoint our personality aspects that dominate our relationship with our partner—to establish how we relate; how much of communications and contacts are driven by Ego, Self, or Model. Especially, when a good portion of partners' demands and attitudes are Ego driven, they might learn how, and how much, they are contributing to the demise of their relationship. They must be fair and unbiased when monitoring their attitudes and roles in undermining each other. Similarly, they should beware of their partner's main personality aspects and learn how they might be causing more alienation and less opportunity to reconcile, often unconsciously and helplessly.

Clearly, it is harder to see and accept our own defects than those of others due to our Egos standing in the way, while we set personal standards of normal behaviour unilaterally, too.

We are selfish in the way: i) we truly believe that whatever we do is right and justified, ii) we use our self-serving beliefs and standards to judge and treat others with prejudice, and iii) we apply double standards for ourselves and others shamelessly. We impose our double standards when we use one criterion to judge ourselves or someone we like, and apply a different one for judging others, especially our adversaries. We are hardly aware of our quirks, anyway. When, on occasions, we notice clues of our wickedness and weaknesses, we find excuses to suppress our thoughts and intentionally support our defective perception of life and our role in the midst of it all. All along, our psychological flaws keep causing deep pains for others and us, as long as we remain not serious or compassionate enough to do something about them.

Nevertheless, we can at least learn that our psychological flaws comprise of, i) those we simply cannot see, and ii) those we face from time to time, but send to our unconscious swiftly in order to justify our desires without feeling guilt or remorse. Even this primary awareness may make us more conscientious and conscious of who we are.

By acknowledging our own and humans' natural quirks we can, i) beware of common psychological flaws that cause alienation, ii) heal our obvious defects, and, iii) handle (bear) our partner's flaws. These three self-awareness objectives are explained in Chapter Eleven (Pages 173-181).

Alienation Preparedness - Factor (Goal) Three

Measuring and Improving Our Tolerance

Without **great** patience and flexibility, we do not last long in a marriage. Most of us learn this fact the hard way eventually. What we perhaps do not fully recognize, however, is that *high* 'tolerance' is an inevitable reality of marriage, a general rule —an absolute necessity. Rather, we perceive patience a major sacrifice and inconvenience (maybe torture) that only we seem to endure. We are actually becoming less patient and flexible in our relationships due to our obsession for individualism and love, misperceptions about the purpose of marriage, and stress from our other life responsibilities. Moreover, we doubt the definition and level of tolerance that can be considered normal and practical in marital relationships. These doubts often raise impatience (and inflexibility) all by themselves.

Another problem is that we mostly depend on our Egos to decide on the tolerance level that feels normal to us—what ego! Usually, during fights with our partner, not only our sour Ego becomes in charge of viewing, analysing, and tackling the issues, but also we depend on this very impatient and selfish aspect of our personality to decide on how much more we can (or should) tolerate the situation. Thus, we hurry for separation and divorce, get entangled in an alienation process, look for a lover, spend most of our time with friends doing things away from our spouse and family, get dissolved in too much work or personal hobbies, become spiteful, etc. In all, a big problem is that we have no objectivity or sensibility to measure our tolerance level realistically. Thus, finding a reliable method to estimate it rather unselfishly for our own good (and for saving our marriages) is a major challenge in itself.

Still, a main test for a couple contemplating marriage is to gauge their tolerance levels—especially their own—carefully and remember that no marriage is safe these days without high tolerance. If partners are not mentally and logically ready for this basic need of relationships, nowadays, they should avoid that marriage at all cost, even if in love. Partners should know how to cope with severe relationship deficiencies, including deep conflicts and quarrels, and still show good intentions and faith, while hoping that mutual sympathy enhances gradually. Many of us may realize at last that most relationship problems remain irresolvable and we must somehow learn to bear them through wisdom. Accordingly, the main questions are, 'Am I the type of person who can go through life in a conflict-laden setting and still make the best of it patiently? Why would I do that?' Then remember our answers forever whenever we face, and suffer from, relationship conundrums.

Tolerance depends on personal virtues reinforced by social norms and partners' level of expectations from relationships. Most of us imagine that a perfect partner and ideal relationship are within our reach and a most natural, valid expectation. We assume tolerance is hardly required, since we can find an ideal companion and atmosphere to nurture our personal needs. With such grand misperception, we do not learn that a marital relationship grows mainly around patience and evolves merely out of flexibility. Our parents and society do not teach us what tolerance means and needs. In fact, many recent social norms advocate low tolerance by pushing independence and equality. We think that *we deserve better*, and that there is something more interesting and joyous out there awaiting us as soon as we get out of our existing marital relationship.

Since partners cannot change themselves fast and easily, their only hope should be to create an atmosphere where they can nurture a *lasting* level of faith and compassion. Tolerance is the platform for building such an atmosphere, within which personality adjustments are promoted and nurtured. Tolerance means letting our partner express and pursue his/her healthy interests. Developing such setting, perhaps as a last resort in some conflict-ridden cases, might in turn goad the process of personal awareness and change. Simply, the idea is that, with tolerance, partners allow each other grow as a person first (and then as a good partner) on his/her own terms, until eventually (hopefully soon) they grasp each other's needs and ways.

On the other hand, tolerance does not mean accepting our partner's abuse or living with a selfish spouse in alienation and isolation. This attitude is more an indication of helplessness and desperation mixed with one's inability, or indecisiveness, to separate. Tolerance is unadvisable for extreme cases where partners are narcissistic or highly incompatible.

Acknowledging the oddities of marital relationships and the inevitable impact of partners' psychological defects improves our tolerance level. We realize why tolerance is a prerequisite of any marital relationship. In this sense, tolerance becomes an inherent product of awareness. It rises in line with the gradual growth of our wisdom, because awareness subsides our Egos substantially and tolerance level is entrusted to Self, which is more patient and passionate by its virtues, but also feels much better the helplessness and limitations of our partner in dealing with his/her defects. We learn to curb our Egos easier, instead of letting it control and ruin our lives.

We can also understand why telling somebody to be more patient or flexible cannot help him/her or the situation a bit. Tolerance is mostly a function of self-confidence and learning how our psychological defects control and render us helpless. Only then, we can raise our tolerance. As an example, at some point, a couple might notice how they always end up fighting when they have opposing views on a subject. They just cannot wait to push their points and save their Egos at any cost. When partners learn how their Egos jump out to control each other and situations, and how useless winning or losing arguments is for saving their relationship, they might become more tolerant of each other's disagreements even when they believe they are absolutely right about something. They learn to just let it go. Soon, both partners reach the same conclusion, if they are not too egoistical, and become less argumentative. Their awareness not only changes them directly, but also stirs an atmosphere that encourages more contacts and communication. This would help partners calm down and realize the silliness and vanity of their egoistic arguments. Accordingly, their attitudes would improve and they would stop insisting on always being right.

A further discussion about ‘tolerance’ is offered in Chapter Eleven (Page 171).

Alienation Preparedness - Factor (Goal) Four

Recognizing Our Opportunities and Fears

A big difference exists between tolerating out of confidence or fear. We are acting from a position of confidence if we tolerate the harsh realities of our relationship based on the 'alienation preparedness' principles noted here. We are monitoring and fighting the alienation process with a logical plan. We remain confident that either the situation would improve eventually, or, when it deteriorates beyond our preset tolerance level, we know how to exit calmly without regrets for not having tried enough or separated sooner. On the other hand, if we tolerate out of fear of unknown future, a less desirable lifestyle, or whatever else, we are only delaying the act of separation while immersing deeper in the process of self-defeat and alienation. In this instance, we are not able to help ourselves, our partner, or our relationship in any manner. The only way to help the situation and perhaps reverse the alienation process is to turn our fears into authentic confidence (compared with false pride). How we can achieve this, of course, depends on the nature of our fears and the strength of our personality.

People's various fears, insecurities, and vulnerabilities are too numerous and peculiar. We must list our own as part of self-awareness. They affect our perceptions of life, decisions, and relationships. Yet, behind any fear, an opportunity awaits to be tapped. For example, behind the fear of separation (and loneliness) stands the great opportunity of finding 'who we are' away from our debilitating urge for a companion. Only we need courage to tap the opportunity that exists behind our fears. If we reorient our minds only slightly to break out of normalcy and the freezing effect of our fears of change, most of us find a new world. We find courage to confront, and go beyond, the apparent limits within our crooked society, thus seize new opportunities. New dimensions of existence present themselves as we embrace the new opportunities. The joy of new discoveries and the relief from old fears would redefine our identity and create a refreshing sense of being. Exploring new opportunities also raise self-confidence. For example, we might have been tolerating our humiliating relationship out of fear of loneliness and inability to find another companion. Some of us in fact prefer an annoying partner to no partner, and we may have a good rationale for it as well. However, behind those rationales could be our weak emotions, lack of confidence, self-pity, and other fears that turn into excuses and justifications. The bottomline is that without confidence we can neither succeed in our present (or future) relationship, nor capture the essence of individualism. We also lose life's vast opportunities, including spirituality, that any intelligent person must explore on his/her terms.

Our doubts about the viability of our relationships intensify our fears—not only the widespread fears of loneliness and emotional breakdown, but also the fears of being wrong in our judgment about the state of our marriage and the possibility of reversing the alienation course. We doubt our partner ever recognizing our needs and being able to provide a chance for a relatively peaceful companionship. We have doubts about the wisdom of staying in this convoluted marriage. We think we should leave our partner before it is too late and we lose our youth and attractiveness. These kinds of doubts and fears can deprive us from exploring the opportunities of making our relationship work in a more creative manner, confronting the alienation process head on, developing self-awareness and tolerance, and possibly saving our marriage. We may suffer from fears of either leaving our partner prematurely or staying too long in a marriage that might never work.

The bottomline is that we may conquer our doubts and fears only by building confidence and faith, and by redirecting our negative thoughts 180 degrees. With authentic confidence built around a humble sense of being, we give ourselves the opportunity for real independence and individualism that lies beyond our fears. We would certainly do the right things when we measure our options from a platform of confidence, with some kind of faith in ourselves and our partner. We would do the right things when we confidently overcome the fears of doing the wrong things *(without getting carried away fast and abandoning a relationship that could have been saved had we just followed the guidelines for 'alienation preparedness').*

After living with a companion for a while, we learn to view life from only one common dimension. We judge our lives' value by the level of our success in maintaining a relationship and a rudimentary career. We ignore or undermine the value of an inherent relationship we (can) have with 'self.' With our fear of loneliness, we deprive ourselves of grasping our inner 'self' that can show us the finer opportunities of life, starting with the recognition of our identity and spirituality. We never realize and utilize our innate potentialities, which can provide us with the greatest secrets of our existence. If only we could bypass our fears of losing our existing relationships or never finding others, we grasp a divine dimension of individualism beyond our customary definitions. This does not mean that we rush out to leave our spouses. Rather, we learn to embrace our relationships with confidence built on full humility and respect them for not only their own values, but also the strengths they could give us to explore our spirits as a supplementary feature of human existence.

The bare minimal benefit of recognizing the inherent power and potentiality in our 'self' is the subtle confidence we gain to repair our damaged relationships through tolerance and wisdom. On the other hand, we should beware of the high chance of growing a false confidence or overconfidence, which merely indicates our neglect to ponder the facts noted in this chapter adequately. Overconfidence demonstrates low consciousness and hidden insecurities that cause intolerance. People's misperceptions about individualism and equality give them a false sense of overconfidence, thus a low tolerance level, while they become more arrogant daily. This misleading overconfidence destroys both our chances of having a good relationship and finding 'self.' It shows our immaturity and neediness. Conversely, authentic confidence makes us humble within or without a relationship.

Thus, we are facing another major life dilemma: Our doubts and fears prevent us from boosting our confidence, and without confidence, we cannot conquer our fears and doubts. It is similar to the trite chicken and egg dilemma again—the old cliché. Most of us grow up with low self-image or often lose our self-confidence during life struggles. As a form of a psychological defect, with our compromised confidence we suffer from our fears and hurt our partner in so many ways, too, including our aggression, suspicions, and low tolerance. Therefore, we must somehow gain our humble confidence to overcome our fears and also apply it effectively to rescue our relationships. Initiating a self-awareness regimen is probably the best way to do that. We cannot buy or learn confidence readily, not even by taking confidence lessons and listening to expensive positive thinking lectures. Psychotherapy may help when pursued for a long period. On the other hand, humble confidence evolves automatically, though gradually, along with the rising level of our consciousness and compassion. This appears to be a much easier and cheaper alternative for gaining our confidence and all the ensuing good things.

Alienation Preparedness - Factor (Goal) Five

Perceiving, Planning, and Playing Our Roles

To suppress the process of alienation, we should play a special role diligently, but first, we must understand our three options: i) just watch our relationship get out of control, ii) aggravate the situation by our retaliations or egotistical manoeuvres, or

iii) decide to play a positive role to prevent it from collapsing altogether. It does not really matter, at this stage, if our partner does not realize or admit in being at least partly responsible for the problems, since any effort centred on blaming or changing our partner's attitude would certainly fail. S/he would probably not even care to comprehend the scope of problems, and thus we would most likely just get trapped again in the same games of faultfinding, arguing and fighting, and challenging each other's Ego. Now, it is time to do something different if we really care. It is time to play a positive role.

The role we should play is different from everything we have been doing so far. The logic is simple and obvious. If we were doing the things right, we would not be in such a mess now, after all. Although we usually think it is only our partner's faults that we cannot get along, we also have doubts about this conclusion in our subconscious and conscience if we just defer to them for a few minutes. In fact, contacting our subconscious and conscience is the first part of the role we must play.

Now, it does not really matter who is wrong or how much, anyway. Those who have blamed only their partners for all the troubles are already divorced! They have convinced themselves of their own perfections and never assumed their Egos were responsible for at least some of the problems. They have also already admitted to the futility of their relationships and do not want to keep struggling and suffering any more.

Often, however, most of us have doubts, since deep down we feel that some of our flaws and attitude (often deliberate actions) inflame raging conflicts inadvertently. Sometime, we might even know and enjoy doing it spitefully with a childish, sly pride! After all, we cannot be perfect, in spite of what our Egos keep telling us forever. Another possibility for still being in a doomed relationship is that we have low confidence and self-image. Alternatively, we may be still too optimistic naively about the chance of forcing our partner eventually to change. Anyway, we often entertain these possibilities, thus reinforce our doubts about our relationships' potentials and viabilities. In all, it does not matter which partner is mostly guilty if we are keen to correct the situation.

Surely, our new role in defusing the process of alienation grows in line with our grasp of our 'self.' Accordingly, it is not too difficult to stay humble and play our marriage-saviour role. We should just be cautious about our approach regarding this sensitive matter, because we are a novice, and because our doubts and fears still linger in our subconscious and make us look hesitant and vulnerable. Still, trying to play a new role all of a sudden, in particular when we have already drifted a long way along the alienation path, is not an easy task. We may feel embarrassed in front of our partner to suddenly appear much softer and more compromising than s/he had ever thought we would (or could) be. Our changes, if real, would definitely come across vividly, even though they may happen gradually. Our efforts to change our personal vision and approach to life (and marriage) would normally emerge slowly. However, our partner notices it at one instance when our attitude suddenly looks different to him/her. We might have even discussed our new ideas with our partner, but it is only his/her perceptions and our ongoing, actual performance that s/he can believe, with some cynicism at the beginning.

Before continuing, the author likes to admit that all these ideas about the role we could play—to curb alienation—sound rather absurd and unnatural. Then again, this chapter's bizarre suggestions actually show how much our pride and reluctance to think and act differently, such as playing a proactive role to save our relationships, have caused us so much extra pains and confusions in life overall. We have been too shy and egoistic to try new ways of helping ourselves and our relationships!

Anyway, we might initially rely on our Model to play the new role, while we become totally convinced of the merits of our sacred mission and become committed to it. Model can be instrumental in containing our Ego until we learn to draw on our Self for facing our partner's persistence to make us fail. S/he might be resentful already of our calmer approach to solve our problems and avoid topics that usually cause arguments and faultfinding urges. Yet, s/he would eventually get used to the new person we have become and most likely appreciate the change, too. Then, s/he might join in with us to make things better, although perhaps not too fast, because of her/his doubts and suspicions as to what we are up to now.

In all, grasping our new role and playing it properly is a big step for slowing down and defusing the alienation process. We accept this challenging responsibility merely with the intention of helping ourselves, and perhaps our relationship eventually. The most important role we must play consists of those steps enumerated about acknowledging relationships' special needs and personal flaws—Alienation Preparedness Factors One and Two noted above. At the same time, our role must fulfil all six Alienation Preparedness Factors (goals) noted in this chapter.

Understanding personal versus relationships needs, setting our tolerance level, and all the rest of it, are vital just to make sure we can play an active role in developing our approach and thoughts for running a workable relationship—especially for finding a more appropriate relationship model. We want to ascertain that when (if) we surrender to alienation, or opt for separation, we have played our role to prevent it (especially considering our own defects). We want to wait until there is no chance of communicating and understanding, although we have set our Ego aside and dealt with our dying relationship only through Self. We realize the need to build our faith and tolerance through a basic commitment and persistence, until 'alienation preparedness' possibly succeed. Taking these odd initiatives is difficult. Yet, showing initiatives is the main idea behind 'alienation preparedness' for growing tolerance as part of the scared role we must play. And only through flexibility, we can best *learn* to give up our egoism and make a good use of our Self. We want to play our role effectively.

People's psychological flaws are too complex and they play a major role in causing marital problems. We all have extreme difficulty in realizing and defusing our idiosyncrasies. Thus, we must admit that high tolerance is an absolute requirement of living with another individual. Yet, we also set a rational level for it based on the characteristics of our relationship and our partner's depth of flaws and goodwill. We realize we are trying to make changes in our approach and attitude by being an active agent of change. More importantly, we should be a true example of change. And, of course, we should understand that most likely we would fail despite our sincere efforts to implement substantive changes. We admit that the alienation process may continue to deteriorate beyond repair despite our good intentions and struggles. We know that our only reward is to make our marital relationship tolerable, if possible, as a last resort. The goal is to gain back our relative independence (in or out of our relationship) without having any regrets later. We want to be sure we have made our best and honest efforts to correct the big mess that marriage partners usually create for each other.

Once we understand all these facts about our role and their wide implications, we set out to implement our thoughts. We plan about discussing some of the issues with our partner, how, and when. We plan about the areas of personal defects that require more care, awareness, and improvement. We plan regarding the required changes that we must pursue actively, personally and perhaps with our partner's help later. We plan our steps, measure our progress, learn from our mistakes, and hope for the best. If necessary, we might revise our plans later and devise more challenging and detailed ones along with our newer refine thoughts.

Playing our role diligently and patiently with compassion would be tricky, but highly essential for salvaging our failing relationships.

Alienation Preparedness - Factor (Goal) Six

Making an Objective Judgment and Decision

To live or leave: That is the doubt!

The most annoying problem in a marital relationship is our 'doubt' about its quality and viability. Should we continue to *live* with our inconsiderate partner, or time has finally come to *leave* him/her? This doubt persists even if we have set proper tolerance criteria and follow the alienation preparedness goals and process discussed in this chapter.

We suffer needlessly when problems (and doubts) remain unsettled in our minds. We recognize this basic dilemma and tolerate it consciously or subliminally as a necessity for social adaptation. However, we also believe that every problem needs a resolution. If we cannot get rid of the problems, we must at least come to terms with them. In fact, it is often practical, and even more effective in the long run, to come to terms with problems rather than solving them or destroying their sources —which often appears to be our partner. We try to accept a problem as an inevitable fact in modern societies when it is not possible to eliminate it. For example, if we learn to see marital problems as a social pandemic, we may be able to take relationship pains less personal. We might learn to cope with them in a rather passive 'relationship model' perhaps, hoping to create a tolerable relationship in spite of its irresolvable problems. The purpose of a good judgment and decision is to settle our marital problems in our minds, especially when they cannot be solved. Ignoring marital problems—on an alienation course towards divorce—appears the fastest and simplest way out. It is a solution, but it is neither a creative remedy, nor an effective way of viewing and settling a problem.

Often problems have no solution, nor can we come to terms with them—like our declining socioeconomic condition, or a wicked, nagging spouse. A major problem might break a person to the verge of committing suicide as the only option for coming to terms with the problem. Or, a terminally sick person might prefer a decent, quick exit to avoid degradation and pain. At the other extreme, smaller problems that remain undetected might cause incessant suffering and stress. We must look deep down in our psyches to find the reasons, and their validities, for our lacklustre life and failing relationships. At least we might realize the scope of our problems, which may be major or minor. Conversely, we may feel that we have problems, but cannot identify their causes on our own.

Another quandary is that no reliable criteria for measuring the degree of our marital problems exist, nowadays. Thus, we wonder if our problems are real or imaginary, major or minor, compared to a typical marital relationship in our mishmash culture. Of course, we might explain our problems in general terms, such as the lack of communication or understanding, but these typical diagnoses cannot help us see the roots of our problems. We could seek professional help and counselling, but at the end, we cannot locate and feel our marital problems unless we make a point of gauging and judging them through self-assessment. We must take on the mission of defusing the alienation process in hopes of curbing the problems eventually and salvaging our marriage. Otherwise, the wisest resolution would be to end the doomed relationship as soon as possible.

Partners could drag a dead relationships on their backs until death do them part. Yet, a tarnished relationship would only stir more sufferings or restrict access to opportunities outside their relationship. We usually realize these facts when we face our doubt regarding an unsettling marital situation. However, before pronouncing our relationship dead, we wish to examine it for any vital sign to ensure no chance of revival exists.

To make a good judgment, especially for such an important decision, we should obviously step outside our Ego barrier and defeat our silly false pride. After all, our impartial judgment regarding marital issues is ONLY for our own benefit, thus we ought to become more altruistic and realistic about the level of personal egoism we can allow for such a serious judgment.

Being a good judge of our relationships is not easy, though. Impartiality is impossible when our Ego is the judge, which is often the case. Ego has become the nucleus of our identity and individuality and the most dominant force in our relationships. It has overtaken most of us to the extremes of perceiving and assessing the world and events only from Ego's point of view. Still, we let it judge and decide for us. We let it control us. In this contaminated environment, it would be extremely hard (but wise) to delve into our true 'self,' at least partially, to mitigate our prejudices and biases.

Then again, some obstacles often blemish our objectivity and judgments about the state and content of our marriage. For one thing, information shortage always raises our doubts about our partner's intentions and the sources of marital problems. Sometimes, we prefer to give our partner the benefit of our doubts, especially if we become partially aware of our own flaws and prejudices. And sometimes we remain optimistic about our partner eventually smartening up and changing his/her attitude and approach. These common erratic perceptions merely raise our doubts and delay our decisions, which we must eventually make.

Alienation preparedness is for helping us curb our doubts as well as our biases by utilizing our newly earned awareness and wisdom. During this process, we collect all the relevant information, including the intensity of partners' flaws and the depth of their *(possibly failing)* good intentions. Then we set our tolerance criteria and level. We grasp and acknowledge our fears and opportunities, and we play our reconciliatory role actively. If we take all these steps properly and faithfully, our judgment is bound to be more rational and impartial.

The first three 'alienation preparedness' factors (goals) noted in this chapter are further elaborated in Chapter Eleven due to their importance for avoiding marital alienation.

CHAPTER EIGHT
Divorce Avoidance

The alienation, separation, and divorce process is too dire and tricky to explain in one book. This chapter's goal is to help readers learn how to gauge their marital options, make better decisions, and boost their relationships in line with alienation preparedness process. The objective is to study the alienation path and avoid the ominous option of divorce.

The 'alienation preparedness' process is for controlling a relationship's rotting conditions that infect partners' judgments, while they stagger on a painful alienation course and struggle with the disturbing thoughts of separation. Through this self-awareness process, we also learn to make our judgments and decisions about marital problems only when we are in control of our thoughts and emotions, and not when we have lost our senses in the heat of arguments. Our judgments are sound only when they are free from prejudices, Ego, and heated emotions.

The Ultimate Options

We must make a *conscious* 'decision' about our relationships now and then to mitigate our excruciating doubts and pains. Our ultimate options are to: i) stay in the relationship and keep playing an active role in defusing the alienation process with patience, ii) stay in the relationship passively and patiently, or

iii) separate. Option (ii) is most common in society, as partners intend to make the best of the current situation helplessly due to their continuous failures or partners' carelessness. The main goal is to salvage our marriages if possible.

We try to choose one of above three options cautiously and *consciously, and then* learn to live with its consequences. We face the same options with or without a valid judgment about our relationship's state. However, with an objective judgment, we are convinced, committed, and play our roles effectively with minimum doubts regarding the risks of the final decision and outcome. Hopefully, we make that tough decision calmly based on a valid judgment about the state of our relationship.

All three options are viable and wise choices depending upon our relationships' conditions, our awareness of the depth and causes of conflicts, and our previous efforts in solving the issues. Each option becomes valid and most viable at some stage of our relationship, but our options get more restricted over time. That is, first we become aware and eager to resolve the problems. Next, we give up and accept the problems as irresolvable, and thus try to live with them without seeing any chance to improve the relationship. We may choose a different relationship model that gives partners more independence in a rather passive relationship. Then, eventually, we may feel that the relationship is intolerable despite our efforts to correct or tolerate the situation, so we choose to separate. During these stages, we are forced to travel fast on an alienation journey towards the separation destination. Yet, we keep struggling—with all our wisdom, conscious, conscience, Ego, Model, and Self to reverse the direction of the demised journey and return to the point of departure, where our relationship made sense.

Intuitively, all of us follow the same order of correcting, tolerating, and quitting our relationships when marital conflicts press. However, intuition would not help if it does not contain a high level of awareness and patience. Our efforts would be productive only when we face these stages with full awareness, high consciousness, and clear conscience through an alienation preparedness process. Only then, we get a better opportunity of resolving our problems, or at least finding a better means of controlling our doubts and making a valid judgment.

Overall, it is unwise to jump to the second or third stages before fully exploring the opportunities that prior stages can offer. We must explore each stage patiently without expecting a sudden change and results, since, most likely, our awareness still needs expanding, and since the process of self-awareness takes a long time to perfect. If our aggravated Ego or emotions push us towards the third stage quickly, without benefiting an alienation preparedness routine, we are bound to make a major mistake that the whole family would suffer from and regret.

No right or wrong answer exists for the question of 'live or leave.' The only criterion is to ascertain we make a *valid* judgment and a timely decision based on the ideas suggested in this chapter. The whole intention of alienation preparedness is to help us with this judgment and decision after recognizing one crucial fact: We are all too hasty, needy, idealistic, and emotional, nowadays, when judging our relationships' health.

The importance of a separation decision calls for pondering many relationship issues and highlighting the implications of many crucial factors. A main goal of alienation preparedness routine is to keep reminding us that we do not have the right mindset to judge and decide properly during a relationship crisis. Accordingly, we need personal faith and resilience to direct our self-appraisal and self-awareness efforts. All along, we try to deal with ongoing crises and make sound judgments without letting egoism and emotions besiege our thoughts and senses during a tense instance. Marriage counsellors might provide some basic advice, but nobody can truly help us make good decisions without our genuine interest, self-awareness, and a sound mindset in line with the 'alienation preparedness' principles.

Thinking Romance and Remarriage

When the thoughts of separation and divorce overwhelm us, it is the best opportunity to awaken our mood of romanticism to put off spite and urges of retaliation that are boiling inside us. This is an excruciating task when partners are on the verge of breakdown psychologically and emotionally. Therefore, even suggesting it may appear pure silly. Yet, the main purpose of self-awareness is to learn control our Egos, then notice our emotions beginning to settle automatically. The question is, 'How to watch our Ego and how to curb it in such a trying circumstance?' One way is to think of our marriage ended and our partner not being around to cause frictions. Creating this image in our heads realistically would feel impossible initially, because of the tension of disagreements and the intensity of abuse we feel our partner has inflicted upon us for so along. Actually, we probably want our partner dead or at least out of our life immediately, *right this minute,* instead of cherishing him/her again like good old days. *"What a weird solution!"* we can yell rightfully. However, with *alienation preparedness mentality*, we might cool down enough to redirect the energy wasted on hostility towards positively charged self-awareness. Surely, these efforts would succeed only if some attraction and *reserved* respect still exist between partners.

At this point, *thinking marriage* is the last logical refuge for us before contemplating the separation option. By thinking marriage, partners assume their present marriage has ended and they are now facing one last chance to enter into a new marriage contract. Except that now partners are wiser, have better knowledge of each other, and do not think that writing a contract would be unromantic. This is clearly possible only if both partners are mature, willing to reduce their expectations, and choose a relationship model that gives them a higher level of independence without tainting the sanctity of their marriage. Nonetheless, at this stage, we do not care anymore whether it is romantic to sign a contract or not. Rather, the whole point is to clarify the practicality and chance of both partners' lowering their expectations from their relationship. We like to assess the chance of renegotiating a contract with our partner in which we can identify our needs, as well as our commitments, before we agree to re-enter into a new marital relationship.

In fact, we might be able to overcome our anger and maybe rekindle some romantic moods. If so, we might think of funny experiences and delightful memories that we have shared, in particular the birth of our children. Instead of feeling pity for ourselves and our wasted lives, we can try to elevate some sense of compassion by recalling our partner's devotions, hopes, and triumphs. We can try to generate creative thoughts about the good aspects of our relationship (past and present) to fathom how inadvertently we have let our oversensitivity and quirks ruin everything. Nobody is to be blamed because this is not the right time for it, and there is not even time for it. Now, it is time to revive the moods of romanticism, if possible at all, to stir some positive energy during this time of crisis. We must somehow reconcile our differences before falling into despair and a self-destructive mindset. To be honest, if no romance is left between partners, so little chance of reconciliation exists, considering the intensity of issues that have carried partners to this level of animosity. Realistically, despite all the attraction and romance, we might eventually feel tired of struggling to save our marriage so many times and failing repeatedly; so it would seem quite logical to quit.

Romanticism at this sad, controversial stage implies mainly compassion driven by plenty of acumen. The mere decision of stopping our spite and retaliatory attitude reflects our wisdom and compassion, which are the bases of genuine romanticism. It does not even have to be expressed or played together with our partner, but felt personally. One way is to recall (perhaps even sarcastically) the romantic memories of yesteryears, then maybe use Model later to share them with our partner even if it sounds rather foolish under the circumstance. The idea is to elude negative vibes, moods, and thoughts, at least for a while. Later, when the situation seems more stable, we might add additional flavour to this simple 'first step' by approaching our partner slowly with passion, awareness, and eventually some novel plans to build a fresh joint life with new principles.

If we cannot elude our negative feelings about our partner, despite our efforts to show compassion and understanding, we have possibly reached the last stage.

Reviving the moods of romanticism in a broken marriage sounds foolish and futile. However, this suggestion is based on the author's own personal experiences and positive results—although a divorce became inevitable ten years later, anyway. From a logical perspective, we can note that, in the absence of any other sensible option but divorce, adopting an unorthodox approach of feeling and expressing romance is our last resort to turn things around, so that partners might hopefully cool down and make a valid judgment. Unfortunately, during these trying times, when marital conflicts feel overwhelming, we usually choose a hostile and controversial approach, which usually only expand hatred and expedite separation foolishly. Only retaliation seems to make us feel good! But we are wrong. It is easy to be a spiteful person. But the art of living is to finally embrace our Self and grasp our sense of selflessness, which automatically revives all the romantic instances of our lives, too, including the ones with our inconsiderate, foolish spouse. It is not hard to change gear and reach for the more tranquilizing emotions of forgiveness and love, if only we can defeat our false pride and disengage our Ego. We can activate our Model to express our raw emotions, if we have a hard time using Self in showing our very deep feelings. Sometimes, we can make a good use of our Model, and this could be one of those precious occasions.

My personal experience relates to the first occasion when my wife and I decided to separate—about fifteen years ago.

Despite our heated power struggles and confrontations, we agreed to see a marriage counsellor on the recommendation of our family physician (after giving us enough medications for stress). The counsellor had an impressive background, with a Ph.D. in psychology and years of experience in marriage counselling. We visited him weekly for about three months and explained our backgrounds, concerns, and our relationship situation. He gave us his professional advice, and we covered many grounds throughout this exploratory and reconciliatory process. At the end, he bluntly announced that he did not think we had a chance. He gave up on us as well! I recall that day very well. We left his office in silence, lost into our own thoughts and emotions. We felt lonely with nobody around to help us, perhaps as a fair judge or mediator, for pinpointing the problems that the marriage counsellor had failed to rectify. The way he had dismissed us felt rude and funny, too!

It became clear to me, at the end, that it did not matter what the sources of problems were, anyway. We are humans, after all, and full of flaws and foolishness. So many things entered my mind, and I realized I had to change my approach, as our only hope. We were getting ready for divorce anyway, so why not give ourselves a last chance by thinking marriage in these dire, gloomy moments of our relationship.

Gradually, I developed new thoughts and options through deeper self-awareness and reading related books. I learned a lot about marriage and divorce. I did not submit to whims and ways of my wife, nor did she to mine. Rather, we made a point to express a basic form of compassion, friendship, and some feelings of romanticism. Especially, boosting romantic moods was not easy for either of us because of our recent negative experiences and our inherently logical (less emotional) minds. In many instances, we drew on our Model to make romantic gestures, which made a positive impact on our relationship, although they still did not appear as sincere as we liked them to be.

With a very rudimentary alienation preparedness process that my wife and I invented gradually, we were successful in reversing the progress of alienation and accomplished the task that even a specialist assumed impossible. We achieved this only by faith and resorting to a more suitable relationship model for us—at least the one I thought might work. I cannot say if we both came to the same conclusions simultaneously or not. But my guess is that one of us played a more active role in propagating the alienation preparedness process without even recognizing what s/he was about to do or achieve. And, of course, both of us quickly encouraged, or at least agreed with, the intentions of the other. Our subsequent relationship was not perfect by a long shot yet. Still, it had improved a lot, from retaliation and spite to a more civilized and romantic approach with tolerance and by accepting the fact that personal defects cannot be defused quickly, avoiding hasty invalid judgments, giving each other more independence, separating our financial affairs, and resisting futile egoistic arguments.

Ten years later, we made another legitimate judgment and decided it was time to quit, and we did. The main question and doubt in my mind is whether we should have separated in the first place ten years earlier. One or both of us may now regret our decision to reconcile, but then (10 years earlier) we had decided that giving ourselves another chance was a smarter decision. We choose our options based on the order suggested at the beginning of this chapter! The problem with life these days is that most of our important decisions do not prove fully satisfactory or effective at the end, for bringing us a relative sense of happiness, or for helping us resolve our fundamental doubts about living. No real solutions seem to exist, anyway, for many of our primary problems! That is life!

Unfortunately, life's major decisions, including marriage and divorce, are irreversible, too. Therefore, our wisdom from these life-changing decisions can hardly help us. Such is life!

PART III

Hardships

CHAPTER NINE
Life's Common Conundrums

Most of people's sufferings in modern societies relate to marital issues or loneliness. Existence routines, including our professions, also weaken our spirits, which in turn make our lives and companionship pains even more unbearable. We face so many disappointments due to our crude ambitions, people's malice, and our increasing needs and expectations from people and society. Meanwhile, our perceptions of marriage prove too whimsical, though we are still expected to demonstrate lots of tolerance and forgiveness for bearing our usually selfish mates besides the incessant pressures for subsistence.

Ironically, we cause most of our sufferings personally for insensible reasons, while our minds' rampant efforts to find practical solutions for this meaningless, confusing life cause us only more distress and disappointments. Actually, merely our childish egoism and misperceptions about life, human nature, and relationships' purposes could be blamed for our hardships. Our growing insecurities, eccentricities, and life expectations have gotten out of hand, while we try to satiate our superficial needs, adapt, and manipulate others with our pompous, fake personalities. Accordingly, our inner conflicts have also grown incredibly, because our naive ambitions and needs hardly get satisfied in our corrupt societies.

In recent decades, we have built a complex life structure around crooked social values that cause too much confusion and frustration. We try to cope and succeed in a competitive, superficial, and showy environment. Yet, this rampant social environment further limits life's capacity to be meaningful, especially for relating to one another. Meanwhile, the amount of social and personal limitations has grown fast, too, thus we feel trapped, unable to define our life purposes or our identities within this mess. Instead of building and staying content with a simpler lifestyle, selfless love, and compassion, we just pain others and ourselves foolishly by letting society contaminate our minds and spirits through crude ideologies and by letting our obsessions for love and happiness deplete our sanity.

All along, life's hardships have diminished our patience and flexibility, while marriages' rising conflicts make our gruelling efforts to survive feel even more absurd. Then, grasping our purpose for *living at all* feels more urgent and relevant every day, too, all in vain, of course. Accordingly, we have become less compassionate, as our senses of helplessness and failure have escalated our alienation within our lousy marriages and lives, thus we rush for separation and divorce prematurely in hopes of finding freedom. In all, our rising expectations from both life and marriage in the new era have crippled our senses for existence, while we are unwilling to acknowledge our own roles and guilt for supporting these gawky, greedy societies.

Ironically, all these growing personal and social confusions mixed with general socioeconomic pressures imposed upon us so casually apparently represent our presumed civilization and intelligence! However, in the end, they merely reveal humans' vanishing logic and sanity!

Clearly, our needs and sufferings are the cause and effect of one another. Humans and humanity are now entangled within a ferocious, self-destructing cycle with no end or remedies in sight! Simply, our unsatisfied needs create suffering, and our rising sufferings induce more psychological needs (mostly for compassion). We all demand a lot of attention, nowadays, to help us through the healing process or at least maintaining a minimal sanity. When we suffer, we *need* some gratifications to distract us or somebody to guide us. Alas, people are also becoming less capable of filling this big void for one another. Therefore, we often end up going out shopping and wasting our time and money on useless stuff!

Our neediness and despair create erratic thoughts, illusions, and pains. Yet, only our thoughts (valid reasoning) can contain our needs and insecurities somewhat. Only the right kinds of thoughts can eradicate our erratic sour thoughts and heal our sufferings. Friendships and consoling can mitigate our pains, too, of course. However, ultimately, we should come to terms with our sufferings on our own through rational thinking. Therefore, the bigger irony is that only we can eradicate our life's hardships, demented thoughts, and suffering with proper thinking. Instead, we only infect our psyches and spirits with more mundane thoughts and deeds purposefully or ignorantly, thus increase our hardships.

Life's hardships compile, since we refuse, or do not know how, to review the deep sources of our sufferings, insist on creating foolish justifications for them, or lack enough stamina for existence. We doubt the triviality of our needs and dreams within the overall scope of the universe. Often, we just blame some imaginary causes or find excuses for our sufferings and self-pity, and perhaps even hope to attract people's sympathy, too. All along, we only cause more pains and adversities for people and ourselves for no reason but the weakness of our convictions and souls, and sometimes out of laziness to take proper actions for getting out of our dire, self-imposed mental slump.

Sometimes, we doubt or deny the causes of our suffering and do not admit that our stress is a symptom of a widespread social problem, i.e., the vanity of our lifestyles. We often ignore our inner feelings (conflicts) that signal the deep-rooted causes of our suffering or quickly turn them into the feelings of self-pity, defeat, and uselessness. Sometimes, we deliberately suppress our thoughts and the symptoms of our hidden problems, e.g., neediness or greed. Sometimes, we let some elusive concepts like love and happiness deceive our understanding of reality. When we doubt our inner feelings and instincts regarding our sufferings, we do not show any interest or motivation to adjust our approach to life and living. Not knowing our true reasons for living, or embracing many erroneous purposes, adds to our sufferings as well. We are usually too stubborn to accept that mostly our naive mentalities cause our suffering, and instead keep pursuing the pervasive values and lifestyles that have proven impractical and stressful. An excellent example is our absolutely wrong approach in marital relationships and still cherishing the same methods and expectations. We cause our own sufferings through our idealistic and whimsical thoughts in pursuit of idiotic social ideals like love and happiness.

Common Sources of Suffering

Although we have unique personal reasons and remedies for our sufferings, most of them have common sources. Learning about the nature of epidemic social sufferings can heighten our awareness and lead to faster recovery. We can learn to manage our pains and paranoia better by pinpointing the insignificant thoughts behind them. Of course, the nature of suffering and its intensity varies according to individuals' outlook on life, sensitivity, insecurities, weaknesses, health, and surroundings. In general, the common sources of mental sufferings relate to some kind of personal needs deprivations, such as:

- Financial burdens and worries
- Social burdens, sexual deprivations, and loneliness
- Paranoia, greed, jealousy, spite, etc
- Psychological defects and chemical reactions in brain
- Lack of social recognition, insecurities

- Personality imbalance due to excessive Ego or Model
- Stress, fears, physical issues, unfulfilled dreams, etc.
- Incomplete or problematic relationships
- Lack of self-actualization and spirituality
- Boredom
- Etc.

Often a few of the above sources mix and cause niggling thoughts and a feeling of mental suffering. The fact that our sufferings are creations of our thoughts does not mean they are not real. However, their intensity depends on our perceptions (thoughts) about their importance, causes, and effects. Merely realizing this fact and controlling our thoughts help us curb our sufferings, mostly by redefining our purposes of living. Moreover, solutions are found easier for most of these causes if we unlearn the conventional methods and criteria of gauging and resolving our problems. We might become a little more creative in circumventing social inconveniences and pressures. What we perceive as a problem might not be a real issue at all within a sensible perspective. Of course, suffering is mostly an emotional reaction, which is difficult to quantify or set a rigid criterion about. Normally, our minds assess a recent situation in reference to past experiences or crude expectations (as our criterion) to establish its intensity. Our conditioned brains do some tricky and hasty assessments before we start to feel the suffering. Thus, we could discard the patterns and directions of our conditioned minds, and instead, draw on our awareness to measure the causes and effects of our painful experiences in a compassionate manner.

We have the option of 'self'-therapy or seeking the assistance of experts to fight the depression caused by our psychological defects, or Ego and Model. All we need is an initial awareness and honest assessment of our weaknesses, which cause our pains. We can help ourselves if we really believe that some *adjustments* are necessary. However, most of the time, we really do not see our deficiencies or believe in our abilities to overcome them.

Obviously, some sources of sufferings are harder to control. This usually happens when brain chemicals and external forces create or reinforce the sufferings. For example, financial burdens are always tangible and possibly due to no fault of our own. Even when caused by our defects such as extravagance or laziness, we still suffer, maybe even more, though at least we could try to do something about it. If we are reasonably aware, and make use, of our potentials to make a living, and do not waste our resources on useless habits or ideas, then our financial hardship is probably not our fault. Or when we have difficulty with our relationships, it is often hard to adjust the situation. In most cases, it is also difficult to get out of them without causing a different kind of suffering for ourselves and others. Still, some alternatives might exist to alleviate the suffering. These kinds of doomed relationships can be worked out with some *adjustments* in the foundation of our thoughts and attitude when the situation itself cannot be rectified. Those adjustments become possible by following the 'alienation preparedness' discussed in this book. Usually couples should find a more practical relationship model to help them interact more productively, even if it must be in a rather passive relationship.

Our sufferings, their causes, and our incessant search for a more peaceful means of living are mostly the symptoms of our negligence to strive for self-awareness and the wisdom of a *'self'-control* life. Once we learn to live under the guidance of 'self,' according to the simple rules of the real world, we would not face as much suffering in our highly demanding societies. We would stop putting too much demand on our partners and relationships in hopes of finding happiness or mitigating our sufferings. In the real world beyond our demented illusions about life, our wisdom would be sufficient to void the sources, and avoid the thoughts, of suffering. We would be able to anticipate the situations, thoughts, and feelings of suffering. We might even be able to turn them around to our advantage in the form of passion and compassion, which are usually the main keys for discovering a few basic things about the big mysteries of life.

We can readily understand and relate to the common sources of sufferings. However, some deep causes of sufferings are due to the deprivation of our inner needs, including spirituality. This occurs when we neglect to place sufficient stress on significant matters of life and to relinquish most of our nonsensical desires, ambitions, plans, thoughts, actions, and decisions that we have been emphasizing on uselessly.

A simple cause of suffering is loneliness. The impression of loneliness hurts many people all by itself, even if they are only slightly ignored or when they are alone just a few hours. They are simply not prepared to bear even temporary loneliness, or even the impression of it. Obviously, many options exist these days for groups or individuals to get together to alleviate their loneliness. However, learning about the positive side of loneliness can curb our fears of it as well, at least partially. During our no-thought experiences, we learn how moments of solitude (loneliness) could be relaxing and educational. Surely, loneliness on a long-term basis is more complex. Yet, we can create some no-thought experiences to inhibit loneliness sufferings, learn self-reliance, and maybe induce higher consciousness and exceptionally divine feelings to bear even eternal solitude.

A major, inherent connotation of the words individualism and independence is the person's ability to *stand alone*, which implies both the divinity and necessity of loneliness as one of humans' precious attributes. If we accept this interpretation of individualism and independence, along with their implications for *standing alone* and *loneliness* stances, we can draw four crucial conclusions: First, we humans have not appreciated and benefited from the privileges of loneliness adequately yet. Second, we have not been able to define and bring an equally divine moment and privilege, similar to loneliness, into our relationships to make humans' sharing moments profound and lasting as well, beyond our short experiences of love and lust.

Third, we have not perceived the words individualism and independence properly, yet brag about and cherish a crooked interpretation of them personally and socially. Fourth, what can we say about the depth and meaning of our individualism if we cannot be independent, stand alone on our feet, and withstand loneliness with grace, if not actually enjoy it?

Probably the most depressing failure of humans relates to their inability to build better means of enjoying either solitude or cohabitation. We have not realized the advantages of these means of engaging our brains and mitigating our sufferings.

Drawing upon the sacred energy and passion that no-thought states or loneliness create, we can satisfy our deeper needs, which automatically generate tranquility and freedom. In such moments and conditions, we can create beautiful things and thoughts that override the feelings of loneliness many folds. The only problem is that our fears and conventional view of loneliness do not let us test and appreciate the advantages of solitude. We have become desperately attached to things and other people, and, as a result, developed this tremendous paranoia and phobia about loneliness. Yet, in the real world, in fact, we are alone and stay lonely, even if we have a house full of friends and family. This does not mean that socializing is unimportant, but rather to recognize the merits of solitude early on in our lives. A more important point here is that the fear of loneliness can be cured only by discovering the joy of many life experiences that erupt only from loneliness and are extremely beautiful and full of passion.

Pain due to boredom relates to the lack of self-fulfilment. It reflects our negligence to find our niche and developing it. We all have some hidden potentials that press us subconsciously to emerge. They demand our attention or else we feel unfulfilled and empty. Exploring and nurturing our potentialities is difficult, of course. However, once developed, they provide a chance for both 'self'-actualization and personal growth, which are the best antidote for our sufferings, too. These adventures are for internal gratification with no other ulterior motives. These experiences fill our lives with joy and creative energy, which would subdue our stress and banal sufferings due to boredom.

If our suffering relates to greed and jealousy, then it should be obvious how we can get rid of it, if only we could develop a wiser mentality. Why do we continue to look for more of the same things, which we cannot consume in our lifetime, anyway, is difficult to grasp. How much wealth and power is enough? We can only ask our Ego! This only shows the absence of a reliable foundation of thoughts to guide our lives.

We can choose a personal life path and develop a sensible mentality away from the influence of our lifelong prejudices and hang-ups. A sound foundation of thoughts surely shows us the need for passion and compassion, strengthening our beliefs, a life philosophy that inhibits sufferings, flexibility, stability, grasping 'self,' and finding the true means of happiness. During this long process, as our wisdom grows, we might gain some insights about life's mysteries, too, as a sacred personal achievement only, but never a fixed, universal interpretation. Nobody can develop a satisfactory meaning for life, after all. Yet, we must take charge of our lives somehow.

Taking Charge of Our Life

Our life struggles have become too overwhelming, because we refuse to adjust our expectations, mentalities, and attitudes. And because we refuse to acknowledge the reasons behind our sufferings, which are mostly self-induced—often due to our naivety about the meaning of life. Thus, only we can mitigate our sufferings by learning to dismiss those insignificant life events and expectations that instigate our erratic thoughts and break our spirits.

Marital skirmishes (discussed in the next chapter) and the big dilemma of loneliness we endure during our passionate search for love (as discussed in Chapter Twelve) are two other big sources of life's hardships that we must somehow resolve in order to take a better charge of our lives. But how?

Enough clues are around us about our misunderstanding of life. We must use them for enhancing our self-awareness, instead of justifying our dogmatism. Our frustration and anxiety often reflect our inattention or misinterpretation of the causes of our suffering. We feel sad because our struggles to overcome our problems seem futile. We feel helpless and lonely, because our search for love and happiness only make us more exhausted and stressed out every day. We try to correct the whole world and to make everybody understand our concerns. We like to inform our friends and family about our failing relationships and neglected needs. However, it seems, the more we try, the less we succeed to communicate with the rest of the world. Our frustrations and anxieties keep rising and we look in the wrong places for remedies. Yet, we refuse to reassess our value systems and adopt a simpler lifestyle, naively believing we have already figured out the meaning and purpose of life.

Another problem is that we look externally for the causes of, and the cures for, our sufferings. We look for the faults of others, things, and systems. We ignore that mostly our own defects, and our persistence to take the perceived world too seriously, produce our sufferings. Our ignorance of our inner powers inhibits our real potentialities to surface and energize our existence, while our thoughts and primary wisdom also lack a strong foundation. Grasping these concepts is difficult for a person who is trying hard to find an honest job and meet his financial obligations, but keeps failing due to discrimination or job shortages. However, if he finds the wisdom of living in the real world, realizes his inner powers, and looks for his few real needs, instead of too many superfluous ones, then perhaps he would stop caring too much about finding a job altogether. He learns to create his own job, accept a lower paying job, or maybe even ponder the possibility of living without a job if he has the psychological power and resources to do so. Anyway, the bottomline is that *ideally* not even joblessness should be a cause for chronic stress and suffering. It must *ideally* induce more creativity to explore other options and opportunities for living and discovering our true 'self.'

We must also admit that our personality and psychological defects create pain and problems for others and us. Personal idiosyncrasies differ according to our unique needs, interests, and willpower. The healing might begin only when we stop doubting the fact that our defects and obsessions are causing most of our sufferings. We should acknowledge our paranoia and hang-ups, and learn how to view, defuse, and cure them. We need the courage and commitment to overcome the main barrier, i.e., our dogmatism and infantile denial of the depth of our insecurities and eccentricities. We have innate lingering doubts about our identity and purity, but fight our occasional wisdom to stop and analyse them.

We should also admit that nobody out there in society is going to change to accommodate us and reduce our sufferings. The chance of finding our soul mate or even a trustworthy companion is also quite low. The odds would not rise if we keep imagining otherwise or dreaming. We should learn to accept, and live with, all these painful facts of life. Actually, we should expect the matters to get quite worse and pressures to mount in the years to come. We must accept the hard reality that no one even understands and cares about our sufferings and real needs the way our imagination desires. Life's brutal hardships would hit us all our lives with very limited, if any, refuge and compassion.

The mere admission of our defects and the causes of our sufferings most likely mitigates the feelings of frustration and helplessness already. The next step is to use this awareness to subdue these deep-rooted causes of sufferings gradually. Only we can adjust our mentality and adopt a more practical life philosophy. We can change our lifestyle and attitude to subdue our sufferings, and maybe even remove our personal defects and desires causing them. We might even be able to stop the alienation process in our relationships, thus bring the highest chance for tasting happiness with our smart, reliable partner in a smooth family environment.

We can develop a profound foundation of thoughts around personal experiences, by studying the visions and prophecies of great thinkers, and by making a finer judgment regarding the truth of existence. We can weed out the influence of social conditioning on our thoughts, logic, and beliefs. We can refute common ideas and perceptions that are senseless. We might even build the spirit and courage to resist the temptations of living and thinking for external approval, sexuality, greed, and power—as they are the direct sources of our sufferings. Then, we can easily refuse to comply with superfluous standards and expectations propagated in society so idiotically.

CHAPTER TEN
Marital Skirmishes

The vast amounts of partners' idiosyncrasies make couples incompatible and incapable of communicating. These common conundrums are complex already, but unique circumstances also evolve in relationships when two people with peculiar personalities come together and try to build a family without having a good sense regarding their being and life in general, including the generic needs of modern relationships.

Therefore, studying the health of any particular relationship becomes too difficult. It gets tricky and sticky to appreciate the depth of issues and find solutions. On top of that, partners are usually too stubborn, dogmatic, and spiteful. These common flaws cripple couples to agree on the causes of their conflicts or possible solutions. The impotency of human logic manifests in full force when partners shrug off all the clear evidences and reasons before them about the causes of their relationship problems. Many books have provided insightful suggestions about marital conundrums for decades with no solid results. Marriages are getting more unreliable and sadder every day, in fact, as we do not know anything about relationship needs and the right factors for gauging partners' compatibility in the first place—when couples still have their chances to make rational decisions. Some irrelevant factors, including loneliness and love, usually make a couple jump into a marriage with great hopes, and then suffer its repercussions for years. Without a viable relationship, or merely tolerating a torturous one, many people suffer their whole lives. The irony is that many simple issues cause major hardships in relationships merely due to partners' naiveté and impatience. Some of these basic causes of relationship hardships are discussed in this chapter.

Communication Hurdles

Communication breakdown is surely a main cause of marital conflicts. While couples seem to understand the content and method of their partner's communication quite well before marriage, they usually have great difficulty communicating after marriage. It is safe to assume that if communication had been lacking or feeling awkward, partners would have wisely not married. If this is true, then something goes terribly wrong after the marriage. Some of the possibilities are as follows:

- While partners may have assumed that they had good (or at least bearable) communication before marriage, they really did not know what communication consists of, and what it is supposed to achieve.
- Many of us seem rather eager to undermine the basic signs of communication hurdles before marriage, or perhaps even dismiss, possibly due to love or loneliness, a few skirmishes that should have raised our sense of caution.
- We all have a tendency to think positively before marriage about the way we know our partners and how clearly we understand the contents and means of our communication. Then we are shocked more every day after marriage when we realize our naive initial optimism. We realize our faulty assumptions about understanding our partner's expectations and the way we grasp each other's simple words, thoughts, and method of communication. Communication breakdowns

are due to partners' misunderstandings or misinterpretations of each other's intentions and needs, of course.

- The level of listening, giving and forgiving, which are all parts of communication, diminishes because partners' initial intentions of impressing (and perhaps manipulating) each other subside after marriage.
- The level of partners' sensitivity toward each other's feelings somehow diminishes, often inadvertently. While premarital communication seems to be tailored for luring our partners, post-marital communication is more focused on domination of the situation and our partners.
- All along, partners become oversensitive and impatient about the way their partner treats them.
- Partners refocus on other life issues, which seem to be more pressing, thus find less time, and need to spend on proper communication. It appears that partners do not pay enough attention to each other's needs and words, though they may continue to be mentally and physically attracted to each other.
- On many occasions, the level of respect declines because partners find out more about each other's vulnerabilities. The idol they had envisioned in a partner proves to be quite defective. The contents, means, and level of communication are, of course, a function of respect.
- Partners often overestimate their tolerance level and put a great level of faith in the power of their love.
- Partners assume they understand relationships' unique needs, but almost nobody realizes the complexities and the rational purposes of marriage, nowadays. Thus, their communication channels collapse, while other marital deficiencies press on and demand some form of cooperation and understanding.
- Partners face family or personal issues and they cannot see things the same way, or they are not prepared to accept each other's conclusions and solutions, only out of spite or maybe

with good personal reasons. Differences of opinions, values, and outlooks make their communications incoherent and unproductive.

- Besides partners' differences in outlooks and personalities, their erratic need urgencies and obsessions often clash and create many additional conflicts in marriage. This wide topic is reviewed in detail in this author's book, *Relationships Needs, Framework, and Models.*

When communication hurdles emerge and we are unable to improve the process, it becomes increasingly difficult to bring it back under control. Some basic communication issues grow into major relationship obstacles where no single issue can be discussed and resolved. It appears as if all other aspects of the relationship have stopped functioning as well. Partners' moods and feelings change and they become suspicious of each other. We stop expressing our needs to our partner, since we find it a waste of time, because not only s/he is not listening, but also our communications are just too cluttered. The things we say to each other sound senseless and against everything we thought we had agreed on implicitly, or perhaps even explicitly, in our earlier communications.

We can analyse our communications to fathom the causes of frictions or our timidity to discuss seemingly touchy issues. We could also observe how partners' insecurities and deprived needs interfere and override their communications' contexts and intentions. Often, communication is convoluted by hidden personal agendas, fears, and other psychological flaws that are unclear or denied to by partners. Under these circumstances, it does not matter what we talk about and what communications' contents are. We usually revert to the same crooked personal perceptions and draw on our deep-rooted idiosyncrasies to express our anger and blame our partners for everything. Any conversation just becomes a prelude to raise the same old grievances. The blames may be well founded or a product of hasty retaliations. Nevertheless, the results are the same as far as communication ineffectiveness is concerned. Unless these basic problems are resolved, our communications' contents, process, and results remain useless.

Clearly, the method of communication influences partners' reaction quite drastically, too. For example, showing interest, concern, and compassion instils a favourable atmosphere for dialogue. It also boosts partners' trust in each other as well as their personal confidence. Of course, this approach works as long as partners appreciate each other's concerns and respect the rules of a good communication process. Acknowledging the conflicts and our partner's feelings often helps the process. Yet, sometimes, one partner keeps raising his/her demands in spite of all the love and compassion that s/he receives from his/her partner—a symptom of severe psychological shortfalls that hinders the chances of improving communication process permanently.

A similar communication hurdle emerges when we think we are giving more to our partner than s/he would ever be able to understand and repay. We believe we are more attentive to his/her needs and show more concern and compassion than s/he does, thus feel deceived and deprived of receiving equal attention and appreciation. In fact, we are quite baffled by our partner's rising demands despite everything we do for him/her already. This feeling of disparity in the level of affection and care by one partner always emerges in the tone and texture of communication and results in chaotic exchanges of charged feelings, instead of productive dialogues.

The problem of inadequate affection and understanding in family relationships is recognized widely. The major remedy prescribed by many books and experts is that partners become more conscious of the situation and show extra affection. This suggestion means that we must make even more use of our Model to produce and present more affection beyond what we naturally feel. We sense a pressure to play an unnatural role, to show extra affection even when we do not feel affectionate for so many reasons. It is necessary and nice that partners see each other's problems and show empathy. Yet, in reality, most of us cannot resolve our psychological hurts by a mere exchange of affection, especially if it feels superficial. Often, one partner's phony show of affection merely boosts his/her partner's Ego and leads to more demands for attention and compliance. This feels and looks like rewarding our partner's selfish demands and manipulations. This might continue even to the point of a full submission of one partner and domination by the other.

In addition, for some of us, the use of Model, beyond what we can genuinely handle and believe in, feels unnatural and torturous. We eventually drop the act or show our discomfort indirectly in other ways in our subsequent communications or outbursts. The big problem is that, even with extra affection, communication deficiencies would most likely keep growing. For example, when the sources of problems relate to partners' personalities, selfish needs, or psychological defects (e.g., Ego, insecurity, and fears), extra affection cannot cure any of these issues in the long run. Despite some tentative improvements, the deep-rooted unrest, demands, suspicions, and other flaws in partners' personalities soon resurface. In fact, extra affection would hinder a chance for logical communication, sometimes.

When our customary communication *methods* result in confrontation, partners feel the chaos and disappointments. Both partners' Egos get agitated as soon as the communication begins, since they anticipate the regular abuse and arguments. The atmosphere creates big hurdles and resistance to tackle the *contents* of the communication, as the method is not reliable and trusted. For example, (A) raises a topic, then (B) interrupts impulsively and makes a hasty comment or correction, which is unrelated to the main content of (A)'s communication. (A) gets upset and tries to correct (B) for unsolicited and irrelevant comment, which then leads to intense arguments and prevents them to really attend to the substantive and pressing matters of their married life. For instance, they agree to discuss their budget and financial plans for the upcoming year. (B), maybe stressed or struck by a recent scruple, reminisces some of his/her past hurts. S/he uses the occasion to relieve the frustrations of, let us say, *about not having enough shoes!* S/he expresses his/her dissatisfaction hastily about (A)'s apathy, inadequate passion, or secrecy, perhaps about the amount of money s/he makes. When (A) asks with surprise for an explanation, (B) replies, "Because you have kept your bank account activities secret." Most likely, other reasons are behind this outburst, but partners' reactions reflect the general mistrust between them. Most importantly, however, the main intention of reviewing the budget is ignored completely.

Therefore, the disagreement over an old, unrelated issue prevents partners to concentrate on their initial intentions and contents of communication. Sometimes a partner might realize his/her rude interjection and/or a mistake in his/her opinion. Yet, s/he does not want to change his/her position due to false pride, or just to prove s/he never makes a mistake. S/he does not want to set a precedent for being wrong even once.

A lack of communication often reflects partners' fears and anticipations of clashes anytime they try to converse. This is the result of many years of negative experiences, and partners' reactionary and defensive attitudes toward all communications between them. Often, impulsive or compulsive reactions and rage disrupt the whole process before partners get a chance to discuss the main contents of their communication.

When communication gets tense, partners only push their ideas and Egos without any attention to their communication contents and other person's intentions or points. Instead, they keep arguing about irrelevant issues only for blaming each other and making noise. In these situations, a possible solution is to enforce a one-way communication method for a while. In this method, (A) explains his/her points, *about one selected topic only,* while (B) only listens and makes notes. Partner (B) leaves the meeting with a grasp of (A)'s concerns, and then spends enough time to reflect on them objectively. If (B) is genuinely interested in improving their communication, s/he can make real efforts to see (A)'s points without getting too defensive and upset. When (B) is ready to go back in a few days with answers and suggestions, this time only (B) speaks and (A) listens without interfering or making gestures to stir unrest and anger. (A) would have his/her chance in a few days again to reflect on (B)'s comments and proposals. This process continues until one topic is relatively resolved. Then to the next item on the agenda, which is prepared by both partners' contributions. In this process, partners apply their negotiating skills, *to solve one issue at a time,* except that they do not talk simultaneously and spontaneously before having a chance to ponder their partner's problems and suggestions.

One-way communication surely feels long and stressful, especially for the partner whose turn is to only listen. The idea of restraining our rage and egoism for a day or two to only ponder our partner's words is torturous. However, for couples with communication issues, but genuine interest to improve the situation, one-way communication method often helps. Its objective is anger management to focus on communication contents, rather than jumping from issue to issue and losing track of the intentions of the communication. The ideal would be to have a third person mediate and moderate the process at least until partners learn to follow the rules of communication and learn to control their reactionary attitudes and anger.

Withdrawal and silent treatment to prevent confrontations might seem the only option to us to reduce our relationship hardships somewhat. In fact, it might prove to be the case at the end other than separation. First, we should try, however, to keep communication channels open as long as possible. If a regular communication method does not work, we can resort to the one-way (rotating) method and make genuine efforts to learn to communicate, as without it any marriage is doomed.

We should embrace this (more sensible) pain (inconvenience) in order to avoid likely bigger agonies that long withdrawals and confrontations cause.

Understanding the depth of communication hurdles and the importance of handling them effectively become even more evident when referring to discussions on page 33 regarding 'Communication and Negotiation Abilities' as a vital success factor and compatibility measure in relationships.

Expecting Our Partner to Change

Expecting our partner to change is another common source of conflict and agony in relationships. When we are young and naïve, we consider our partner's declaration of love *a kind of* submission to (or at least acceptance of) our way of thinking and living. Immediately, we assume that not only we know each other, but also love would motivate our partner become the image we have of a perfect spouse. Thus, we get married. Initially, we expect our partner to guess and understand our thoughts and needs and adjust her/himself accordingly. We expect change in all matters and levels. We want change of attitude, thoughts, beliefs, dress code, words, relationships and friends, etiquettes, eating habits, things we desire or dislike around the house, the way and time we choose to do things, our philosophy and outlook on life, political views, tastes in things, on and on we can add to the long list of our whims! All these idiotic thoughts and wishes run in our subconscious as a hidden human trait, anyway, even if we do not admit it.

When this does not happen automatically on the power of our love per se, we finally lose our patience and *ask,* politely, directly, through subtle manipulations, or sneaky retaliations, for some changes that we believe are overdue. And, again, when we do not witness true changes, we become anxious and angry with our partner for being so stubborn and unwilling to cooperate (change). We *demand* change or try to manipulate our partner to get the results we need and reduce our pains. Especially, as our insecurities emerge, e.g., when one partner gets possessive, s/he would demand her/his partner to change drastically and stop being too friendly, charming, or flirtatious around other men or women. This is usually a big challenge when some people do all these things on purpose merely for raising their partners' jealousy or as retaliation for some other conflicts in their relationship.

In all, our first mistake is to assume that the strength of our love would subdue our partner's natural resistance to change. Our second mistake is our assumption that s/he can change and is merely resisting it deliberately. Mostly the appearance of resistance and apathy towards our requests and expectations agitates and frustrates us. Therefore, we keep getting into vain arguments. Naturally, we also blame our partner for being the cause of these arguments, especially for refusing to admit his/her stubbornness amidst many other growing faults.

However, the fact is that people hardly change, since their personalities are shaped mostly by their unconscious urges, which drive them to be who they are. They cannot control even their thoughts and attitudes, which are driven mostly by their subconscious minds. Only sometimes we can draw upon our Model to portray an attitude of change, merely for social adaptation and acceptance purposes. Yet, this tentative change fails to stabilize and we revert to our original form soon, since change is not internalized and we cannot subdue our old habits and needs. Permanent and stable changes require some major psychological incentives or deep personal convictions through experience and enlightenment. We do not change since others ask us to, and not even by a mere personal choice, but only because our wisdom and convictions have reached the level in which real 'change' brings the truth we trust.

Our unrealistic assumptions and expectations for 'changing our partner' lay the foundation for many marital conflicts and pains. If we admit change is never automatic and controllable at the level we desire, we can become a little more empathetic and flexible with our partner on this matter. We must not only evaluate our intentions for expecting our partner to change, but also remember they cannot do it readily even when they work on it very hard. Then, we might stop attributing our partner's inability to change to spite or purposeful resistance. Of course, some personality adjustments are possible, even at noticeable degrees, when a person keeps his/her Model at full alert to play certain expected roles. However, these changes are most likely fake, and the degree of change is not fundamental. In all, personal changes are simply unattainable without a full intention and a long process of self-awareness.

Why Do We Expect Change?

We want our partner to change for many reasons. For one thing, we desire a routine that is convenient for us, or because our partner's habits, values, or ethics bother us. Another reason is our strong tendency to dominate others and make them do things our ways. Most of us have strong inner urges to control events and people. We should dominate others or else feel dominated and overruled. We attempt to change our partners' personalities to make them more subservient, dependent, and agreeable to our frame of mind. We imagine we can save our marriage only by making our partner change, and to ensure the situation does not get out of hand. Another strong reason for demanding change is our 'need for feeling loved and testing our partner's devotion.' It satisfies our urge for possession, too. Our partner's dependence on us (for love) gives us a sense of security (because we feel wanted, needed, and a sense of being in control of our marriage). We need to be *spoiled* to curb our insecurities. Sometimes, a person is simply psychotic and just likes to test how much s/he can push his/her partner!

We also demand change obsessively to satiate our need for ELove. When our partner refuses to change, our Ego feels threatened and our need for being loved feels under attack. All along, we think we are honest and true in terms of our love for our partner, while s/he seems more careless every day. 'Love' and 'being in need of love' are different concepts, though. While 'love' is a mythical expression of beauty, devotion, and giving, 'being in need for love' reflects our selfishness, needy attitude, and humans' innate urge for dependency. We think love, but in fact are influenced and driven by our selfish 'need for being loved'—to be spoiled, as a new fad in relationships.

Thus, we take our partner's inability to change to heart, as a sign of not only his/her vindictive persistence to contradict us, but also not loving us anymore. We keep thinking s/he resists change only because s/he does not care about us enough, and not that s/he cannot change. Love and need for love are good topics for understanding the self, ego, and model aspects of our personality. Even when we attempt to invoke our Self and inherent spiritual need for love, often Ego interferes with its 'need for love.' All the expressions and pretences of love are reflections of Model manifesting the feeling of love without really grasping the true implications of selfless love. Clearly, all three aspects of personality reflect some type of love when we express or demand it, but it is mostly Ego driven.

Sometimes, we may try, or pretend, to change to make our partner happy or show that we care. Therefore, we activate our Model to portray the change. We force ourselves to make the best use of our Model to display a change of attitude. We do it for a while, but most likely fail to bring about a real change. Model is the least stable aspect of personality and forgets its promises, and in fact has very little tendency in concerning itself about commitments. It can be swayed easily by strong incentives to adopt a different position or role, or just drops an existing one when Ego begins to interfere. When we cannot keep our promise to change, our partner becomes even more furious and takes our apathy as a further insult and rejection of his/her love. His/her anger reflects how his/her need for love is threatened, thus causing him/her suffering. Our partner takes the broken promise as a rebellion, retaliation, or loss of love depending on the circumstances.

Overall, we hope love and marriage per se give our partner ample incentive and power to change. Our egoism and naivety force us misjudge our power and the possibility of making our partner think and act according to our life outlook. We believe if s/he loved us enough, s/he would change to prove it. We like to gauge our partner's capability and sincerity in his/her declaration of love and devotion. Thus, we expect her/him to change immediately, often drastically. If s/he does not, we take it as a sign of her/his inadequate devotion and commitment, if not sudden hostility and rebellion altogether.

Why Cannot We Change?

We cannot really detect and control our Ego easily in order to affect a real change. We may change our attitude a bit, mostly temporarily, but not our essence, which comprises our way of thinking, convictions, habits, preferences, pride, etc. To prove this point, we can refer to experiences when we faced our partner's retaliation for something. We may recall how quickly we reverted to our Ego despite our effort to reflect an 'attitude' change. We got angry, even when our Model had meant to keep us tactful, or our Self had meant to be compassionate and understanding of our partner's inherent flaws. This shows that 'attitude change' is often a superficial act with no substantive meaning and conviction for the person displaying a change. Meanwhile, our inability to change makes our partner angry and disappointed. S/he concludes that, not only we do not love her/him, because the change is not internalized, but also s/he has been fooled all this time by our phony display of change. Thus, relationships deteriorate further by partners' tentative and shallow changes. The only exception is when one partner undertakes such basic changes as steppingstones to explore new avenues for helping his/her marriage, which might then lead to self-awareness and essential change slowly. Tentative attitude changes are helpful in calming turbulent situations, but partners must know why change cannot be deep unless it occurs gradually through self-awareness, personal conviction, and experience. We should not depend on our partners' fake changes to satiate our 'need for love' or as a measure of his/her real 'love.' These tentative changes are unreliable, and their depth and purposes are highly questionable, though they might be useful for stabilizing relationships atmosphere.

An interesting scenario usually occurs after we go through a few rounds of temporary changes without success. In our next round of negotiations for change, we decide and demand that this time we would compromise (change) only if and after our partner has portrayed authentic changes first. We expect our partner to prove that his/her change is real and permanent before we adopt and show the changes s/he is expecting from us in return. Interesting and comical enough, hardly anybody agrees with this demand. This scheme (threat) cannot motivate us to change, anyway. In a similar scenario, sometimes, we do not discuss or demand change with our partner explicitly, but ponder privately the chance of changing our attitude in some respects if our partner changes his/hers first in the areas of our desire. These scenarios show our high frustration with broken promises, so resorting to desperate means of bargaining. These situations, which often sound very much like blackmail and threat, prevail as a last resort when partners lose their trusts about each other, at least for effecting change.

Promising to change, but more so hoping to convince our partners to change, happens quite often in the early stages of relationships when partners try desperately to salvage their marriage. On the one hand, the mere intention to change (by one partner promising to change first or both partners doing it simultaneously) reflects their sincerity and deep desire to make their relationship work. On the other hand, it shows how hollow and naive our promises for change can be and how little we know about the possibilities of change. It also shows our struggles to push our Model as much as possible to portray a change that we do not believe in truly, or cannot control. Sometimes, partners consent to a mutual change of attitude, while they do not like the demanded changes in principle, anyway. They usually call this a compromise. However, deep down, they might not be convinced of the purpose and value of their efforts. They are only agreeing to change (cooperate) just to get something they need or merely to calm the situation, but not that they believe change is good for them personally, or even for improving their relationship. The effect of this kind of compromise is discussed in the next section.

The Effects of Demanding Change

Considering partners' inherent resistance to change, often their intention to compromise, for the good of their relationship, leads to over-activating their Models, which then affects the other aspects of their personalities indirectly, too. We do this in social and organizational relationships as well as marriage in order to cope with tough situations and to accommodate others. Our influence over one another has both positive and negative implications. A positive impact happens mostly when Model strives to show compassion, and maybe overcome Ego eventually, and perhaps even internalize that compassion as a deep 'self' trait. It means, under this special circumstance, the individual really grasps and believes in the *purpose* of change and practices it with an open mind and heart.

On the negative side, we often begin to resent our partner and marriage even more when playing Model is solely for the sake of stopping our partner's nagging. Increasing our Model requires a comparable reduction of either Ego or Self. Ego is rarely reduced, and it occurs *only* when change is internalized in the long run as an accepted target for improving personality.

Thus, our integrity and Self is sacrificed most often in the form of lower 'self'-esteem, and 'self'-image, when we keep playing a sharper Model without believing in our efforts as a right attitude or thought. As long as a change does not feel essential (in our mind), we know that our shallow 'attitude changes' are bound to collapse when we get tired of playing a role, find other priorities, or revert to our real personality and let Ego rule over the Model again—as it normally does and feels more natural, too.

Another side effect of using Model regularly is that it must be constantly kept active and alert, or it would lose its focus and momentum. For example, we may inherently nurture a lot of love in our Self, but are unable to express it freely. Thus, we exploit our Model to express love as part of a relationship therapy. This therapy makes us attentive on the surface, but the process feels odd and contrary to our agitated nature and integrity. Therefore, we feel an inner conflict and tension. An added problem is that, after a while, our partner's expectations get used to our new attitude and heightened level of attention to her/him. Our improved attitude may soon appear inadequate to him/her again, so s/he makes new demands for even higher attention, while we feel pressed to play our Model too much. If we forget only once to express our love in a particular and timely manner, it would again be conceived as a loss of love.

As another conundrum, when marriage partners take the position that 'change proves love and love justifies change,' they are only abusing this belief subconsciously. That is, they mostly want the change in their partner, instead of themselves, at least for becoming less demanding and selfish personally. Accordingly, they impose extra burdens on their marriages and communication, and thus raise both partners' sufferings in their relationship due to their misperceptions about 'love' per se helping or stirring people to 'change.'

The rules of relative success in marriage are not hard to discuss, but are difficult to believe in and implement. The first principle is to not make foolish assumptions, especially during initial courting and evaluating our partner, regarding partners' potential or motivation to change. Second, often only tentative 'attitude changes' could be expected from 'our demand for change,' at best. Real changes can merely happen from within a person and not through an outside force or someone else's demands. Third, love and being in need of love are different phenomenon and neither of them can play a role for change. Only our misunderstanding regarding the relationship between 'love' and 'change' is causing so much hassle in marriages. Fourth, we must focus on changing ourselves to understand and accept the relationships' needs in the difficult environment of the new era. Finally, remember that relationship conflicts arise mostly when one partner tries hard to change the other, knowingly or inadvertently, while the other feels pressed to change without being genuinely motivated to change. Why change anyway, when the reason for change does not feel natural. Deep down, a resistance and inner voice says, "I do not want to (or cannot) be like you or anybody else." Knowing that change cannot be easy, we should revise our degree of premarital optimism and stop hoping that we can make our partner change. Even worse, we would be too naïve to believe marriage by itself make our partner change for the better to make us happy or boost our relationship, anyway!

Some interesting suggestions in John Gray's book, *Men are from Mars, Women are from Venus,* might help men and women adjust their attitudes and become more acceptable and pleasing to their partners. On the other hand, the above points about the instability of 'attitude change' suggest that we need a fundamental technique to bring partners closer together. We need changes in relationship mechanisms, to induce sensible commitments between partners naturally (instead of relying mostly on role-playing just to get along superficially, while raising each other's frustration and inner conflicts). We need only one major change in our common mentality: To grasp the role and needs of relationships in the new era. Although men and women seem radically different mentally, they have the same basic need for companionship—as their most urgent and essential need. Although men and women might seem to have come from different planets, the only way they can come to harmony and peace is by inventing and grasping a common language. Sometimes, it seems women have become homesick, perhaps due to so many years of exploitation by men on this confusing planet Earth. Thus, now, genders have real difficulty grasping each other's language, especially for all the growing ambiguities that modern lifestyles, role-playings, and social values have imposed upon us. For any possibility to resolve the existing marital conflicts and miscommunications, better relationship guidelines and a common language for genders must be invented. Perhaps we succeed in a couple of centuries or so! That is, if women have not already returned to Venus, *which could be one kind of a solution. Or maybe we could send men back to where they came from!*

The Ultimate Frustration

Eventually couples reach the conclusion that their whims for changing their partners and building a relationships environment of their liking are futile. They feel defeated and their frustration shows in their attitudes. They try to cope, but cannot stop nagging and blaming their partners for everything, usually without any direct cause for doing so. They do it merely to relieve themselves from their lingering frustrations and agonies. Partners lose trust and respect for each other, and instead feel spiteful regularly. Their ideas and suggestions usually erupt in hostile tones and their marriage turns into the battleground for firing blames and nagging at each other. Having a marriage partner appears to be the most convenient way to relieve our tensions. However, the outcome may be devastating over time when partners get carried away with all these 'tension-releasing' schemes unconsciously.

Partners' blaming and nagging attitude might be either a deliberate or an unconscious reaction, but either way, they soon exhaust partners and their relationship. Ego drives this attitude with no sign of Model's flexibility to soothe even the elementary frictions that erupt in any relationship. Naturally, Self is absent when nagging and blaming goes on. Ordinarily, using Model helps in expressing one's sufferings and needs in a more passionate and convincing manner, in hopes of stirring some tangible, productive communication and possibly some sympathy. However, with nagging and blaming, we lose the opportunity of showing our honest feelings, through Model or Self, to keep the situation under control. Overall, blaming and nagging reflect our inner sufferings due to either our failures to change or manipulate our partner or our unrelenting need for attention.

Partners' frustration and spite further provoke their need for controlling and dominating each other somehow as well. Our urges for domination of family life and our partner obviously reflect our inherent frustration for our inability to manipulate our partner. It reveals our intention to control the decisions, actions, and behaviours of all family members. We need to do this in order to ensure things proceed as we think is best for all. We might even have the good intention of salvaging our relationship from going the wrong way. Yet, mainly, we wish to control our destiny and independence as much as possible. When our needs for control and independence are threatened by our spouse's objections and interferences, we see the need to dominate the situation and our spouse quickly. We do not want surprises, risks, and headaches. We like everything to proceed smoothly as we have planned personally and perhaps with input from our parents or friends. We simply feel a need to control family issues and situations. However, when we find out that our spouse likes to influence those same issues and situations, we are left with no option but to control our partner as well. Therefore, the logical tactic in our minds is to control any situation and person that may affect the outcome of our plans and expectations for a kind of life and relationship we prefer in line with our zeal for personal independence. We expect our partner to grasp and accept our values, perceptions of life, and logic. We believe our principles are most logical, thus everybody should agree with them after we explain them to him/her, often in our crooked language, anyway. However, if they like to resist, we plan and persist to remain in control somehow, or else we get agitated and retaliatory all the time.

CHAPTER ELEVEN
Alienation Awareness Accents

The first three 'alienation preparedness' factors discussed in Chapter Seven require a higher level of 'self'-awareness, thus accented in this chapter based on their importance under:

1. Managing Our Tolerance Level (Factor Three)
2. Coping with Human and Relationship Flaws (Factor Two)
3. General Relationship Issues (Factor One)

1. Managing Our Tolerance Level

Setting a *level* for tolerance that is meaningful and reasonable to us based on our relationship's specific conditions is a major task for 'alienation awareness.' No scientific rule exists, but two guidelines can help: 1) Never set the tolerance level (and apply it) during a crisis, and, 2) Remember that, nowadays, couples have much less tolerance than is natural and needed for an average relationship. Our rising romanticism, obsession with individualism and identity, and stress have made almost all of us less patient, so we begin our relationships with low levels of patience, tolerance, and compassion.

Having a preset tolerance level means that we have taken our time, have used our wisdom to evaluate our relationship rationally, and have grasped its strengths and weaknesses. It also means that we always lean towards reconciliation, unless we have calmly and rationally arrived at the decision that we have *well* past the preset level of tolerance. As a customary approach, setting the level of tolerance is a matter of balancing the merits of our marital relationship against the conflicts and headaches it causes. Naturally, it is hard to gauge and balance the evils and virtues of our relationships. Moreover, tolerance cannot be a matter of equilibrium between good and bad stuff in our relationship, but rather how much abuse we can take without hurting our health and stifling our souls.

We should develop good criteria for *presetting* a tolerance level that is logical and workable for a particular relationship. These criteria depend on each relationship's characteristics in terms of its merits, but also partners' intelligence and goodwill to improve their attitudes and method of relating. In particular, we should disallow daily turmoil and disagreements rule or change our tolerance level and mood. Instead, the criteria must be set only by reviewing our relationships' merits objectively. We might adjust it occasionally if some major facts make it necessary to re-evaluate our marital situation.

Tolerance and confidence are the prerequisites (and also the cause and effect) of each other. They reinforce each other within a person. As a confident person, we develop tolerance against opposing views and arguments of our partner without feeling our Ego humiliated. And with tolerance we learn more about our Self and our relationship in a rational way, thus gain more control of our attitude and situation. The rational control of our emotions in our relationships enhances our confidence directly even further.

Having an objective tolerance level helps in several ways. First, we become immune against Ego's interference during a crisis and forcing hasty or illogical decisions. Second, we maintain a rather high standard to measure the impact of any crisis against it and assess the health of our relationship. For example, we do not allow our spouse's frantic disagreements turn into a major crisis when, for instance, the issue is whether s/he spends too much time with his/her friends. During such arguments, partners' Egos usually get too aroused and their tolerance levels diminish. Thus, the trick is to ensure partners' brains do not rush in to reset their tolerance levels during a few seconds (or days) of extreme rage. They must learn to make a judgment only after cooling down and weighing the issue against their objective tolerance criteria.

We have Oscar and Emmy prizes for people acting in some fictional and frivolous roles, yet neglect to acknowledge the wisdom and level of tolerance that people must extend to act in real life just to make their marriages successful!!

Misinterpreting Tolerance

Then again, sometimes, our partner may misread our tolerance as weakness and submission to his/her demands. Although this misunderstanding should not affect our attitude, we cannot let it linger and dominate our relationship. If our partner misses or ignores our divine intention for saving our relationship, s/he would never appreciate our tolerance, nor make any efforts of her/his own. At the same time, bragging about our tolerance causes negative reactions, since it might sound we are doing our partner a big favour. That is actually exactly what we are doing, of course. We are doing ourselves, our partner, and our relationship a favour, but our partner would not appreciate our insinuation. Thus, we must present our tolerance to our partner in a subtle way. (Gosh, how much work and diplomacy is needed, nowadays, just to maintain a basic relationship!)

As noted before, the purpose of tolerance is to create an atmosphere of cooperation for eventual change of attitudes and approach. If one partner is not involved in sustaining this environment, the other partner's efforts would not help much; besides growing his/her own wisdom and tolerance, of course. In addition, our partner might in fact keep increasing his/her expectations and demands, instead of adjusting them, if s/he does not recognize the purpose of our tolerance. Thus, while we are working hard to mitigate the sense of alienation, our partner may be completely off the track, pushing his/her own personal agenda, or maybe even testing our limits.

Overall, we must be firm in our communication and show our intentions of tolerance *tactfully*. Yet again, our hints must not sound like a threat or a sacrifice. Rather, we should portray our good intentions to make our relationship joyful for both of us, because we care about it. We do not only express our good intentions and convictions, but rather demonstrate them in our actions. We should be nice while showing confidence, mainly by curbing our emotions, both positive and negative ones.

If our partner appears to be taking advantage of, careless about, or misinterpreting our tolerance, we should rethink our options more carefully. We make a decision that serves us best personally, i.e., to accept the situation and tolerate some more or go for separation. For the former option, we should create a personal approach and atmosphere for some kind of mutual cooperation and communication, even if it is a rudimentary (passive) approach. We might even need to give in a little at the outset. If we can create an atmosphere to convey our initial thoughts to our partner, we may eventually find an opportunity to discuss the concepts of alienation preparedness, tolerance, and cooperation for saving our relationship. If we conclude at the end that no such possibility exists, the only thing left to do is to project life under these substandard circumstances and the chance of a miracle turning things around. Then decide.

At the end, we are responsible for the tolerance level that makes sense to us. It is important to believe that the whole idea of tolerance is for our benefit only, not our partner's. All our efforts are solely for increasing our objectivity, though our partner and our relationship benefit as well if the alienation process is slowed down. In fact, the 'alienation preparedness' routine must be viewed as a personal attempt to learn about life and relationships without expecting other rewards. Well, perhaps the only other reward is the likely redemption of our marital relationship and raising our chances of enduring a life with a person who, in most cases, cannot think, feel, and act the same way we do.

2. Coping with Human and Relationship Flaws

By acknowledging humans' pitiful nature and our own unique quirks we can, i) beware of simple psychological flaws that stir alienation in marriages, ii) heal our obvious defects, and, iii) handle (bear) our partner's idiosyncrasies better.

i) Beware of Humans' Simple Psychological Defects

Fortunately, the psychological defects of majority of us are not too extreme to require specialized attention and cure. We are mostly inflicted with minor, simple defects. However, sadly, these defects, such as lying, deceit, rivalry, and greed, have become an inherent part of our personalities and manifest in our dealings through Ego and Model. They are deep, negative personal traits and emotions that occur too often, like the ones listed in the 'Simple Psychological Defects' in Table 11.1.

Table 11.1: Personal Defects Causing Alienation

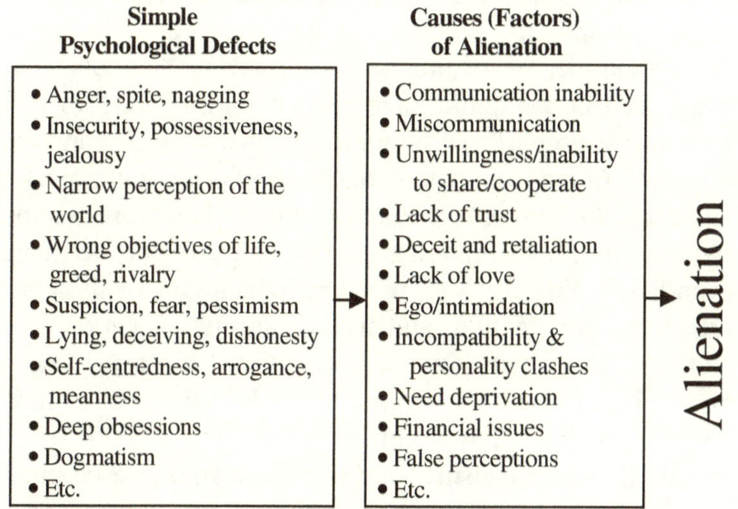

Clearly, any one or mix of the simple personal defects in Table 11.1 can turn into many factors of alienation. Of course, alienation has other causes besides psychological defect, too. For example, a misunderstanding or a partner's weakness in expressing him/herself can cause miscommunication, although they are not psychological flaws. Yet, even small irritants and weaknesses may lead to deep alienation issues.

Mentioning a real story about weakness in communication may help here. It happened when a woman asked her husband a question:

One Sunday morning, an unexpected snowfall had covered the streets and driveways. He is in the middle of a job when his wife interrupts him and asks about his plan to shovel the snow in the driveway. It is around one p.m., snow has stopped, and it seems to him that it may rain and clear the snow in the driveway. He looks at her with surprise and asks her, "Why?" The confused wife replies, "Because we have to go to work tomorrow! If you don't, it might freeze overnight and make the driving out of the garage difficult in the morning."

To avoid needless arguments, he agrees, "Yes, ok. I will do it later this afternoon." Only when she leaves with stress, he realizes the weakness of his communication. Without telling her his reasons, his wife did not have any clue why he was resisting the idea of helping her, *like usual,* so she took it as a blunt rejection. He could have instead said, "Yes, I will. But let's wait for a couple of hours to see if it will rain and clear the snow." Often, we try to economize in our communication, or assume our partner can read our minds. Therefore, a simple weakness in our communication can cause major, permanent misunderstanding for both partners, which can easily lead to further retaliatory actions and arguments, and alienation.

On the other hand, we do not always have a presence of mind and excellent communication skills to be precise enough in our interactions to avoid misunderstanding. Even if we did, it would be too exhausting and time-consuming to be precise with all our communications all the time. Therefore, we must always remember that what we hear and understand from our partner's comments is most likely not all the facts that s/he had meant to convey. We should ask for clarification calmly when the message is not clear enough to us or sounds weird.

ii) Heal Our Obvious Flaws

If motivated to do anything about our psychological flaws, we can start with those we already know about and face regularly. For example, our senses of rivalry, jealousy and selfishness are easy to spot in our feelings and encounters. We can remember these basic flaws in our conscious mind and witness them jump and interfere in our marriages and decisions regularly. Thus, we can tame them a bit; though eluding them fully needs super power. Yet, we normally find an excuse to quit our chances for learning! We forget our commitment to monitor and assess our behaviour in an unbiased manner. For example, if we are jealous, we blame it on our partner who instigates it in us.

It feels more natural to us to control others—in this case our partner who makes us jealous—than to control our own defects. For one thing, we consider our partner's behaviour provocative, which raises our doubts about his/her intentions or innocence. Is s/he a devil or merely a gullible? Since we cannot control our doubts (or misperceptions) regarding her/his intentions, we try to control the source of provocation and our doubts—our silly partner. After all, if we did not doubt his/her intentions, we would not be suffering rowdily about everything s/he does. Anyway, regardless of her/his intentions, wicked or innocent, we feel the urgency to relieve the cause of our pain in the quickest way—by controlling our partner. As another obstacle for learning about our defects, some of them—e.g., competition and greed—have become such a prominent part of our personality, nowadays, they manifest as fully inherent and normal behaviour beyond our control. Heck, the whole society propagates them as valid norms and positive traits.

Thus, we manipulate and hurt others in different ways, e.g., through rivalry or out of greed, instead of acknowledging the personal defects we seem unable to control.

Yet, many of these so-called norms (defects) are reversible habits acquired through social conditioning. Our experiences, humans' cruelty, and societies' general unfairness, sometimes even by destiny and God Himself, make us quite cynical and callous. Yet, our seeming helplessness is not completely true.

Although receiving professional help is wise, we should mostly depend on ourselves to learn about our (and humans') defects. Realizing our obvious defects and those still hidden gives us a chance to defeat them slowly. We can try to find the strength to control and turn things around. The only trick is to believe in our inner power and the possibility of drawing upon it once we get serious and sincere to detect our deeper flaws.

The significance of our attempt to learn about our defects and fighting them is in *the way* it improves the quality of our lives and relationships. Conversely, our relationships offer a good setting to explore our defects, while we can test our new convictions in the way we relate to others less selfishly. We learn about not only our defects, but also their effects on other people, especially those we seemingly care for. Thus, we learn about caring and showing compassion, too. This would be the beginning of a self-cleansing and soul-searching endeavour, which brings much higher value and rewards beyond the basic benefit of controlling our defects.

The way we eventually view and judge our own, *and then other people's,* defects is also crucial. Instead of blaming and paining ourselves and others for all these psychological flaws, we mostly blame human genetics and bad experiences, though we all can try to defeat this barrier to enter a healthier lifestyle past our existing routines. We can view our efforts to curb our defects a healing process, which might expand our lives and minds to such heavenly planes beyond common imagination. In fact, we could take a negative aspect of our lives and turn it into a soulful exercise of tranquility and beauty. How easy it is to grasp the meaning of real life, and yet how hard and painful we have made it for ourselves by letting simple flaws like Ego and spite deprive us of appreciating the sanctity of our spirits. We could forgive ourselves, instead of merely ignoring our defects. Once we focus on forgiving, instead of forgetting, our defects, the healing process begins.

Acknowledging our most obvious flaws, and their direct impacts on our minds and souls, also provides a chance to test our willpower and wisdom. Mitigating those direct, constant sources of our suffering, such as rivalry and greed, gives us enormous strength and tranquility to challenge our deeper, less obvious, flaws. Our awareness of our defects, and our attempts to tame them, avails the opportunity of finding out more about our 'self' and learning to live within its boundaries naturally. Accordingly, our new wisdom and vision of our 'self' makes the alienation preparedness process smoother and easier.

Acknowledging our defects does not threaten our identities or raise our psychological insecurities, contrary to what our challenged Egos want us to believe. It only opens a window of opportunity to gauge our inner hurts and insecurities and delve into our deeper nature after working out our most common and clear flaws. Thus, we gradually get into the deeper aspects of our psyche, explore our 'being,' and fight the devil that stands between who we are and who we want to be. We would also gather the courage to accept input from our spouse about any of our flaws that s/he can see, but have remained hidden from us. By the power of our soul, we would stop rejecting the information that flows readily through people's view of us and about how we hurt others. We would welcome the information, because we now have ways of assessing its viability and value to us without getting too offended and defensive. We listen to people's comments open-mindedly, although they may be, and often are, wrong. Yes, we still perceive and keep the right to make unselfish, fair, and compassionate judgments regarding others. Observing people's normal hang-ups and attachments make us feel sad about both their obsessions and helplessness to live in such a phony world. However, all these observations only make us more patient and compassionate with reserved temptation to preach them, in spite of our big reservations for their idiotic lifestyles and mentalities.

iii) Handle (Bear) Our Partner's Defects

Only after recognizing the depth and dangers of our defects sincerely, we might gain the objectivity required to assess our partner's psychological flaws as well. However, our view of his/her flaws is now only a compassionate exercise and vision. We see those flaws as debilitating factors largely outside of his/her control, although s/he is somewhat aware of a bunch of them for sure. Our basic challenge is to recognize our inability to do anything about our partner's flaws directly. We can do something about ours, but not his/hers. Thus, our analysis is merely an 'alienation preparedness' exercise for assessing our ability to cope with them. We hope a natural transformation in her/him make our lives easier, which we believe can happen under rare circumstances through personal life experiences. In all, instead of blaming and trying to change our partner, we become more understanding of people's difficulty to control their flaws. We can play a role—noted in Chapter Seven—but our expectations differ from what we have had before delving into these analysis. Our awareness is merely for re-examining our marital expectations and controlling our anger and anxiety. Therefore, we suffer less personally, cause less pain for our partner, and find more energy to take productive initiatives that often produce the same results—mainly peace—that we were after in the first place, i.e., when we were struggling hard to change our partner to accommodate our needs.

Knowing the type and extent of our partner's shortfalls and their impacts on us is useful *only* for improving our judgment and tolerance level. The goal is to become fair and objective in our judgments about her/his intentions and control over his/her attitude. This knowledge can help us mitigate our doubts about the viability of our relationship and build tolerance, at least for a short while, without always making a fuss quickly about our partner's conflicting personality and flaws. The question is how much efforts are required on our part to live with relationship flaws without blaming or arguing with our partner about them indefinitely. That is, since s/he cannot change, how much time are we willing to devote to saving our marriage before asking for separation? The next question is whether we have played our active role properly to mitigate alienation. If there is, in our minds, any time that we can spare to view things from a different perspective, before asking for separation, then that may be the most productive time in our marriage, hopefully.

With our new approach in dealing with our partner and her/his flaws, s/he notices our 'attitude change.' This would be a basic positive step in reversing the process of alienation. By curbing our nagging or criticizing, our partner would put down her/his guard, too. Then, we use our energies to appreciate the new opportunity opening up in our relationship. S/he would try to fathom what has made us change our attitude and approach. This provides a chance to apply the one-way communication method or similar mechanisms to voice our concerns logically without pressing our expectations or asking him/her to change. We discuss only issues that hurt us or weaken our relationship. Our change of attitude and rising patience most likely show in our sincere, diplomatic approach automatically.

As noted above, we might have a chance do certain things about our partner's defects without aiming to change her/him. We can *indirectly and tactfully* raise our partner's awareness about his/her psychological defects, their dire impacts on our relationship, and the ways they are reinforcing the alienation process. We do this in many ways. For the most part, showing our non-blaming attitude and patience would lead to positive reactions, in most normal people, in time. 'Patience' implies (and may need) waiting for some months or even years before its significance can be established in our spouse's eyes. Yet, this level of awareness and patience (waiting) would by itself change us and our expectations as well, in terms of viewing and handling relationship conflicts. Accordingly, even minor compromises by our partner starts to appear quite vivid and pleasant. Then, with our subtle acknowledgement of his/her efforts, more tangible changes might follow, as s/he might find them satisfying and rewarding, compared with the old method of demanding and whining.

Most improvements would be slow and little, yet a move in the right direction and must be recognized and encouraged, so that partners feel their good efforts and intentions are noticed and appreciated. Waiting for ultimate outcome before giving feedback and support would cause further alienation, since our partner's efforts per se are valuable even though the result may not be apparent for a long time, and because defeating his/her defects is such an excruciating task to accomplish. Partner (A) would perceive (B)'s lack of feedback a sign of (B)'s apathy or a sign of (A)'s futile efforts to change, which seem to have no tangible outcome on their relationship. We do not have to get into a formal expression or appreciation of the improvement. In fact, doing that might have adverse effect on some people. Rather, we should give our feedback by implied gestures of appreciation and perhaps an emotional reward as simple as a warm smile in a proper moment, or an invitation to a romantic dinner at the right mood and time. Then, making some hints, maybe indirectly, can also help. Nevertheless, exchanging feedbacks regarding positive changes in each other's attitudes help the 'alienation aversion process' a lot.

Our efforts help us directly, and we can help our partner indirectly by our attitude, but also by introducing her/him to alienation preparedness process when s/he appears ready to listen to our experience. The ultimate success comes when both partners begin to trust each other's judgments about their personal and relationship's weaknesses, especially the ones causing their alienation. This would help them recognize their less obvious flaws gradually and overcome their doubts and hesitation to admit them. We cannot necessarily get rid of our defects because we have acknowledged them. Both partners know that and take this barrier into consideration with respect to their dealings and expectations from each other. However, the mere attention to our flaws, especially knowing that our partner is also aware of his/hers and acknowledges them, at least slows the process of alienation, and instead transcends us to a level of understanding and compassion, then the healing, and finally the effective control of personal flaws.

3. General Relationship Issues

No 'normal relationship' exists in society anymore. Therefore, couples must especially recognize the nature of the following areas of potential risks in their relationships:

- Marriage environment
- Main alienation sources in relationships
- Partners' (in)Compatibilities

The effects of these major causes of relationship problems are noted throughout this book, but more details are offered in this chapter, as they demand partners' high vigilance.

i) Recognizing Marriage Environment

Relationships should be viewed as an independent entity with many unique needs. In reality, however, everybody imagines that relationship needs must be an extension of their personal needs. They believe their relationships should satisfy a large variety of their personal needs and also bring them happiness. These are erroneous expectations and assumptions. In fact, it is the other way around: Partners are responsible for satisfying the specific needs of their relationship first, before it can fulfil even a few of their personal needs in any way. The topic of 'relationship needs' is quite extensive and explained in this author's book, *Relationship Needs, Framework, and Models.*

After learning about relationships' unique needs in general, partners should also establish the *unique needs* of their own relationship due to partners' personalities, needs, sensitivities, aspirations, etc. The goal is to raise partners' grasp of potential issues and situations that stir concerns and misunderstandings between them in their unique relationship mainly due to their irritating idiosyncrasies that might infect their relationship fast. Do they know if and how they might defuse those very likely problems? They must also grasp and believe in success factors in relationships, as explained in Chapter Two.

Recognizing relationships' needs and peculiarities is not a casual exercise, but a lasting commitment and responsibility. This includes understanding alienation risks and developing an alienation preparedness mindset to maintain a sincere and peaceful relationship atmosphere. Partners' efforts to share their thoughts and commitments with each other are also vital for several reasons. First, by discussing the contentious issues (and alienation preparedness goals), we show our partner how seriously we feel about our relationship and how patiently we should work together to fulfil our *sensible commitment* to our marriage. Second, dialogue per se enhances teamwork and friendship. Third, through dialogue we might be able to raise our sceptical partner's interest about the benefits of 'alienation preparedness' and perhaps joining in with us more actively to make it a permanent facet of our relationship.

As our main role and responsibility to develop a functional relationship environment, we must know and show 'how much we care' about our marriage, and feel our apprehension about alienation destroying our relationship. Simply, we must grasp sincerely the importance of a serene relationship environment, and then commit to developing it before it loses its momentum on an alienation course. Yes, relationships should build and maintain a momentum rather than being left alone to dry out or get sluggish. Knowing the consequences of alienation can help us focus on the task of finding out 'how much we care.' Still, we often have some doubt about 'how much we *really* care.' We have doubts about the quality and viability of our marriage.

Worst of all, we have doubts about 'how much we care about our spouse.' We might actually care about him/her, but we do not know 'how much.' We do not have a standard for measuring our level of 'caring.' Therefore, we often trust our emotions, which are either too soft or hard, but also tentative and driven based on our recent perceptions of our partner, in particular after our recent skirmishes. We do not know how our 'caring' can, or should, translate into a reliable measure of tolerance of our partner's defects.

We often gauge our affection for our partner intuitively by comparing him/her with people we naturally love, like our children or parents. Accordingly, our spouse usually gets a low score on that scale, which then heightens our doubts about our level of caring for him/her, the purpose of our relationship, and our options. Especially for people who crave love keenly, their mediocre caring about their partner feels inadequate and a cause for concern. We always crave to love someone and also be loved in the way it manifests in our wild imaginations. However, an authentic sense of caring is different from, and does not necessarily require, love, but mostly compassion. Anyway, the more realistically partners care for each other, the more actively they care about keeping their relationship atmosphere peaceful.

Usually when couples separate temporarily, because one partner goes on a long trip or perhaps lives alone after a fight, they get a chance to figure out how much, and why, they care about each other and their relationship. Then again, we do not know whether this caring, during our partner's absence, is our reaction to loneliness or passion for our partner—perhaps a little bit of both. This knowledge is valuable not only for the information it provides about 'how much we *really* care,' but mostly because it encourages us to learn 'why we care,' by measuring the *content and features* of our relationship. We must know why we care about the health of our relationship with this particular person.

After we learn 'how much we care and why,' we like to know 'how much our partner cares.' This is even a harder task, because it is difficult to imagine what goes on in our partner's mind. Even when our marriage feels faltering or out of steam, most of us still give our partner the benefit of a doubt and find some sorts of excuses to justify the signs of his/her random apathy. (This is because we wish to believe that we are still being loved and lovable. And, sometimes, just because we need him/her so badly.)

On the other hand, some of us are overly pessimistic about the health of our relationships. We misinterpret our partner's slightest impatience and neglect as a sign of carelessness and apathy. Then this misunderstanding affects our image of our relationship and partner. However, many reasons might exist for our partner's seeming carelessness. We can strive to figure out the truth behind the appearances, i.e., his/her actions and behaviours, if we care. Anyway, for pursuing our 'alienation preparedness' objective, we should initially establish whether both partners genuinely care for their relationship and each other, regardless of what their words and appearances might suggest.

Another important factor to learn regarding relationship environment is that different types of relationship models are becoming prevalent, nowadays, to fit our modern lifestyles and odd personalities. It is wise to study these models and adopt a suitable one according to partners' personalities. Instead of dreaming about an ideal relationship that satisfies all the needs and aspirations of both partners, a more liberal relationship model, where partners have higher independence, can often minimize alienation and increase the health of a relationship. Discussions about relationship models are also extensive, thus the readers are encouraged to learn more about this topic in this author's books, *The Nature of Love and Relationships* or *Relationship Needs, Framework, and Models*. Overall, the idea is that, with the higher independence of partners, their expectations from their relationship are reduced, thus partners would not interfere with each other's personal affairs or get on each other's nerves too much all the time—a rather obvious and prevalent option in many relationships these days!

Naturally, it is difficult to boost a relationship adequately without both partners' cooperation and while one of them is highly careless. However, it would be even harder to interpret the meaning and purpose of our partner's indifference about our relationship and the ensuing painful alienation. His/her indifference feels like a major blow in our face any time we attempt to assess the flaws of our relationship. It may be a sign of her/his indifference toward us and our ideas of any kind, including self-awareness and alienation preparedness processes.

Often one or both partners remain careless, because they do not know how to go about discussing relationship needs calmly and objectively. Sometimes, our partner may appear careless because s/he has lost faith in our abilities to reconcile our differences, or perhaps s/he has even lost interest in our marriage altogether. S/he might have lost his/her trust in, and respect for, us. However, apathy may be a sign of frustration, since her/his efforts to prevent alienation do not seem to be effective, perhaps because we are not responding favourably to her/his efforts to fight alienation, or just because we do not understand his/her approach or meaning.

Carelessness might be a sign that our alienation has grown beyond repair. It can also be only a mask, an artful Model presentation, for a partner's hidden inner turmoil and conflicts.

S/he may be angry, jealous, or insecure about the events that surround our relationship, but plays a careless role in order to protect his/her Ego or to avoid futile skirmishes. Sometimes, showing indifference is just for drawing the partner's attention to oneself or towards unresolved relationship conflicts. Thus, the trick is finding the right source of our partner's apparent apathy, which might include one or more of the possibilities noted in these pages.

Another scenario might be that our partner cares enough about our relationship, but does not feel necessary, or does not have time, to get involved in alienation preparedness routines. Impatience or time shortage is usually the commonest and simplest source of apathy. Surely, if we can convince him/her to join and share the responsibility for alienation preparedness, the odds of success increases drastically. However, convincing our partner usually proves to be a frustrating challenge. On the other hand, if we constantly face our partner's resistance to participate, we should eventually decide whether and how to fight alienation alone. The mere fact that our partner does not cooperate or share responsibility for enhancing our martial relationship pushes us into a state of isolation and alienation. However, that is not necessarily a reason to give up yet.

It is possible that our partner has already reached his/her conclusions. Maybe s/he thinks we have already travelled so far on our alienation journey that discussing marital problems would not help. Sometimes, one partner does not share his/her concerns and expect the other to understand her/his meanings automatically and maybe even show some kind of concession. And, sometimes, the excuse for his/her silence is that s/he feels rather ignored or that their communications have often led to arguments and useless fights. Anyway, when a partner refuses to discuss his/her opinions, the process of mutual awareness is hindered. Then again, to grasp the depth of our problems and assess the process of alienation, we eventually need to receive our partner's reactions and feedback in order to assess our position.

Our partner's seeming disinterest to participate actively in the process of awareness and alienation preparedness confuses us. It is frustrating to keep guessing various reasons for it. Is s/he quiet because s/he is agreeing with some of our suggested solutions, thus silently and gradually changing her/his attitude and approach? Is it because s/he is not willing to accept our suggestions out of spite, or only trying to avoid giving us a reason to brag about how right or smart we are? Is it because s/he is careless inherently and we are wasting our time and breath? Is s/he in complete disagreement, but afraid to say so because of possible retaliation? Or, because s/he simply does not want to get into arguments and useless awareness efforts? Would not s/he have become more enthusiastic and spoken up already if our efforts were working? May be yes, may be no! Nevertheless, making both partners believe in the *value of alienation preparedness* for keeping a peaceful relationship environment is ideal, but often unrealistic.

We normally stress on the importance of communication for keeping the relationship atmosphere open. Still, mostly the underlying *awareness* property of communication makes it so crucial for preventing alienation. Communication without the objective of 'learning and acknowledging' would be mostly a waste of time and a cause for more arguments and conflicts (which is another form of losing sight of relationship unique needs).

Sometimes, communication is just for the sake of creating joyful moments to share with our partner. A more important aspect of it, however, is to encourage and develop a relaxed environment while partners enhance their awareness about themselves and their relationship. Conversely, if partners communicate with the goal of 'raising partners' awareness,' their relationship environment improves drastically, too. For example, one-way communication to listen to our partner's concerns and needs can be considered an awareness-oriented exercise. However, we must grasp the gist of the information we receive through listening to our partner's words. Naturally, our communication should have some useful content and goal. We should try to grasp the root of his/her concerns. Are our Ego, insensitivity, and careless attitude hindering the sincerity of our relationship? Or, is it mostly those unfounded demands and whining of our spouse that make us alienated and unable to communicate naturally? Often, it is a combination of both. Or, perhaps the mechanism of communication has been weak and caused these side effects.

ii) Acknowledging Alienation Sources

Many issues start an alienation process, but the tentative list presented on page 102 is useful for pinpointing the most likely sources of problems in a relationship. Some events, situations, and behaviours in any marriage usually point to one or more of those main alienation factors and a variety of smaller issues. Together, these alienation sources complicate the mood and content of a relationship beyond the bearable standards that partners had imagined. Partners get confused, lose track of the real sources of their problems, and sometimes quarrel over trivial matters idiotically just out of spite. Even when those minor conflicts are resolved, partners quickly find something else to nag about all the time. Deep down, they are often quite apprehensive about many irreparable conditions and do not like to even think about them, such as their loss of love and respect for their partner.

Often, a seemingly small irritant might, in fact, reflect a big problem, while some of partners' naggings may be only small excuses to conceal major problems in their personal lives or relationships, e.g., when one partner is having an affair. In all, studying even small incidents can help us learn more about the deeper issues in a relationship. Some minor arguments might indeed be symptoms of one or more larger problems hidden or ignored all along, most likely due to partners' inabilities to find workable solutions for them. Meanwhile, even unresolved small problems can gradually turn into a major alienation source in a relationship. Through awareness, partners might learn to become more sensitive about the issues that require emphasis, while fussing less about intangible ones.

Some marital problems could become overwhelming and we simply cannot resolve them, so we ignore them, hoping they would go away by themselves. Meanwhile, we continue to suffer their consequences, while approaching marriage breakdown, too, because we refuse to take a firm action. For example, a gambler or alcoholic has a major problem without him/her admitting to it, or worrying about its consequences on his/her marriage until it is too late to do anything about it. The difficulty lies in pinpointing and admitting to problems that demand immediate attention from amidst the bulk of trivial issues. Often, we create new problems for ourselves and our partner just for avoiding the main one. We waste most of our time and energy on faultfinding, retaliation, and creating more headaches for each other. Therefore, we hardly get any energy and motivation to deal with those few major problems of our relationship. When our minds are preoccupied by blames and demands all the time, no incentive or creativity exists to work on the main problem.

Again, we should remember that 'alienation preparedness' is an ongoing process. It is developed gradually and leads to incremental wisdom about our relationship and ourselves. We cannot expect to identify our relationship's main problem(s) and recognize its circumstances and flaws quickly. Rather, we can find better explanations and solutions for our alienation problems only by spending time and efforts to learn about the intricacies of all relationships these days. We also learn about the requirements and needed resilience to pursue the learning process objectively and gain the required wisdom to save our marriage.

Once the main problem(s) are identified and brought into a high level of consciousness, our tensions would subside, even though the problems are not resolved. Merely the knowledge about the real sources of relationship conflicts relieves a great burden from our shoulders and reduces the stress caused by confusion and a sense of helplessness. The process would be more productive if both partners agreed on the sources of their problems. Then, by focusing on major problems, they become creative in finding solutions, or configuring the hidden causes of problems. They realize that a mix of major and minor issues often causes complications, conflicts, and alienation.

Studying alienating sources in relationships often points to partners' unique psychological defects, which were discussed earlier in this chapter. Yet, a typical situation, which usually leads to conflicts and alienation between couples, happens when partners go through a period of cool down—may be a few days of withdrawal—until a specific or subtle mechanism brings them back together. Most often partners' sexual urges push them to reconcile. One partner usually takes the first step, though, not based on who feels guiltier or needier for sex, but rather his/her psychological vulnerability during that specific period. On the other hand, a partner might have a stronger, forgiving personality, thus take steps towards reconciliation. His/her goodwill and intelligence goad him/her to work on their relationship conflicts proactively and wisely, instead of letting alienation ruin their relationship due to partners' false pride and dogmatism. Anyway, a sense of power struggle and domination often prevails in most relationships. Perhaps it is not intentional, but this inhibiting condition ruins relationship atmospheres somehow.

Partners' psychological vulnerability fluctuates according to their daily experiences and predicaments. For example, when a partner is unemployed, struggles with office or health issues, etc., s/he feels mentally weaker than normal. His/her depleted confidence and yearning for affection make him/her vulnerable to all kinds of abuse and manipulation. During such times, this partner is usually subdued and eventually forced to initiate the makeup process after every fight or even small conflicts. This approach eventually leads to resentment about self for being such a loser. Conversely, one partner may wish to have everything under his/her control, to the extent that s/he may even create a fight only to humiliate his/her partner, just for enjoying his/her partner's defeat and maybe even getting a direct apology. S/he is usually attempting to justify and affirm his/her position about their marital conflicts while refuting his/her partner's viewpoints.

Only an alienation preparedness process can help partners realize the vanity, unfairness, and destructiveness of their games and approaches. They might develop a sense of fairness and learn to become less dogmatic for reconciling their regular skirmishes. They do not even need to agree on a mechanism for reconciliation, as it happens automatically while grasping the intricacy of their relationship. The main goal, of course, is to disallow a variety of inevitable conflicts between partners linger too long and lead to alienation.

The best reconciliation mechanism is when partners try to use a combination of taking turns and using their conscience to initiate a reconciliation path during a cool-down period. The trick is to realize and respect each other's needs for building his/her confidence and self-image for, and through, boosting their relationship. Through 'alienation preparedness,' partners learn to enhance each other's confidence rather than exploiting a partner's diminished spirit at a specific time. They appreciate how humiliating it is for a vulnerable partner to become also a subject of his/her partner's apathy and blackmail.

The above noted simple cases prevail in most relationships, but partners are not aware of them or do not know how to deal with them. Unfortunately, our own psychological needs and insecurities cause these small problems or misunderstandings and quickly turn into fundamental sources of alienation. Yet, partners' incompatibilities also cause a great deal of hardships in relationships, as discussed in the next section.

iii) Recognizing Partners' (in)Compatibilities

Knowing the areas and levels of their compatibilities is crucial for partners mostly before marriage, but they should also keep working on them forever. The compatibility measures reviewed in Chapter Three would be useful, although some specific tests are needed as soon as possible. In particular, pinpointing major incompatibilities is important to avoid marriage, despite their attraction and love. Even minor incompatibilities might cause conflicts, so partners should at least learn about them and get ready to somehow handle them effectively if they still wish to risk marrying. Actually, more incompatibilities always emerge only after marriage when unexpected couples' eccentricities surface. Still, even some advance knowledge and preparation with open minds for these possibilities are crucial, even when partners are compatible in some other areas. They should learn how to draw at least on the strengths of enough compatibilities to offset the burdens of their incompatibilities somewhat in line with an elaborate plan for teamwork. They also need immense wisdom and willpower to choose at least a relationship model that might curb the risks of their incompatibilities—most likely by keeping partners' dependencies on, or expectations from, each other at a lower level.

Recognizing and using partners' unique qualities are crucial especially for teamwork. The time and effort partners share for this exercise would by itself enhance their relationship. Yet, in most relationships partners do just the opposite. That is, they waste their energies on finding and criticizing each other's weaknesses to boost their own Egos, manipulate each other, and control their relationship. They exhaust and depress each other, instead of grasping and applying their compatibilities or complementing qualities needed for teamwork. They retaliate, instead of learning the benefits of teamwork and eliminating rivalry between them. They do not appreciate or merely ignore what each partner can offer to maximize the synergy in their relationship.

Obviously, if partners do not have enough compatibility and unique personal qualities to offer, they should have not started their relationship to begin with. More importantly, if they have major or irreconcilable incompatibilities, they must not marry on the premise that their conflicts would be resolved or tolerated *somehow*. Nevertheless, the goal is to implement ideas and methods that promote their compatibility, while they stay vigilant about the areas of incompatibility, which demand partners' attention and sensitivity. Learning to draw on their compatibilities is vital for bringing order into their relationship more consciously and proactively, and for curbing alienation.

After gauging their strengths and compatibilities, partners must eventually participate in objective (unbiased) evaluation of both partners' flaws and weaknesses that often hinder their use of their compatibilities and cause alienation—mainly due to partners' miscommunications and egoism. The focus is on personal flaws, however, in the sense of trying to recognize and resolve *our own idiosyncrasies,* instead of striving to find our partners' and criticizing them. The alienation preparedness process requires our conscious efforts to beware of the causes of miscommunication, as explained in Chapters Nine and Ten.

Finally, partners must stay vigilant and proactive, while working on their relationship needs as a routine practice of one's life. At this point, the task of awareness per se, is kept in partners' highest level of consciousness. The main objective is to keep ourselves abreast of our commitment to 'grasp marital needs and contentious problems.' Yet, this general awareness affects other aspects of our lives, too, including self-awareness. We can develop a 'marital awareness checklist' that reinforces our logic, purpose, impartiality, and agility as a routine task for both cohabitation and self-development. Some items on this checklist may look like the following:

- Separation is mostly the outcome of a sneaky alienation process that reaches a boiling (no-return) point unexpectedly.
- Only partners' knowledge of the alienation process and clues can prevent their relationship from falling into this trap.
- Alienation is a process that sneaks and grows gradually, so watching for its symptoms with great diligence is essential.
- Partners must be proactive and play certain roles (Factor Five discussed in Chapter Seven, page 121) to elude alienation.
- Repercussions of alienation can be severe, even before it gets out of hand and leads to separation.
- Alienation is mostly caused by partners' psychological flaws, yet misperceptions and miscommunications increase alienation fast.
- Many simple issues and judgments can cause alienation.
- Partners must be ultra conscious of the ways they convey, receive, and interpret their communication, including their tone of voice.
- Partners should be careful in the ways their oversensitivity and false pride may cause alienation and negative reactions.
- Without due sincerity, objectivity, and fairness, partners cannot stop the process of alienation.
- Etc.

Without alienation awareness, we cannot make a conscious judgment about our relationships, thus have difficulty making rational decisions. We remain doubtful about many variables in our relationships and our options, until our partners force a decision on us, or we make an irrational decision in a moment of distress and Ego attack. Naturally, these types of hasty and emotional decisions are disastrous and we should avoid them as much as possible. Especially, if we feel we are reaching the end of the alienation road, we should remember that this is our last chance and the right time to **think of marriage now that it appears like the time of divorce**.

CHAPTER TWELVE
Love and Loneliness Dilemmas

Love and loneliness cause major life dilemmas for almost everybody, since we seem helpless in choosing a viable option for living and loving. We simply do not know how to relate effectively, nor are we trained to live independently. Instead, we are fed with all sorts of fantasies about love and filled with the fear of loneliness. Our dependency on society and work organizations for subsistence and services already jeopardize our self-image, while our financial needs compete with our self-realization and independence needs. Then, our love and companionship needs stir an even higher level of dependence and desperation. At the end, a big variety of our conflicting needs create many personal dilemmas for us all our lives.

Right after earning our sense of independence from our parents, we find ourselves in need of loving and being loved. Sexual drives intensify and complicate the matter even further. Therefore, before we really get a chance to test and enjoy our independence, we are drawn into other sources of dependence, like love, attention, and companionship. We feel our need for dependence even before we actually meet somebody or build a relationship. The mere sense of loneliness and our growing need for companionship weakens our whole image of being and freedom. After we meet somebody and actually begin a relationship, the level of dependence grows even more. While trying to face, and nurture, our feelings of dependence and love, our inherent need for individualism—as an independent, assertive person—keeps imposing another set of deep inner conflicts. Moreover, our struggles to distinguish, consciously or subconsciously, between our love needs and sexual drives become an added source of pain, confusion, and doubts.

Anyway, our desire for independence and our inevitable submission to our urges for love and sex turn into a disturbing dilemma throughout our lives. We struggle all along to solve this dilemma by fixing (and balancing) our feelings somehow, helplessly and uselessly. While we feel more in control with a sense of independence during some periods, we soon revert to our need for love and the feelings of dependence that come with it. For either love or sex, or simply eluding loneliness, we must depend on somebody else who is willing to share similar feelings or experiences with us. Our relationships need mutual dependence and understanding in order to stabilize. Without some degree of commitment and integrity, relationships do not last or take the required form to satisfy both partners' needs for a companion. All these requirements create a major paradox in our personal lives, but also across the society.

Our ceaseless failures to satisfy our need for dependence or independence cause psychological shocks and depression. For one thing, we start to doubt our identities and 'who we are' without a companion. We doubt our sense of love and urge for companionship, while we wonder about the effectiveness of our approaches to find and manage them. We start to doubt our abilities to fathom our preferences and options as well as our knack for living independently. We get entangled between our erratic emotions and lousy logic fighting forever.

On the one hand, our doubts could be a blessing under the circumstance, as our raw logic or emotions often cause havoc for us, including the risks of hasty decisions, such as a sloppy marriage. On the other hand, our stressful doubts during our perpetual dependence-independence cycles and the sense of helplessness in decision-making are not easy to handle, either. These innate, conflicting needs and feelings are painful, as we wrestle with the endless headaches of relationships in society and wonder about couples' failures to relate these days, despite their haunting obsession for a worthy companion.

All along, our fear of loneliness competing with our deep urges for individualism and independence cause lots of pains and depression—the outcome of our loneliness dilemma.

Marriage and companionship are the biggest sources of lingering doubts in life, because both options of living alone and with someone else cause us pain and stress, nowadays. Sometimes, loving someone makes us feel even lonelier when we cannot relate to him/her effectively and often feel helpless and unappreciated. This endless source of doubt and stress is a reason why marriage has become a major life decision. Our warranted doubts and cynicism about relationships, and the effects of dependence-independence cycles, reflect the failing state of relationships and the rising intricacy of our basic need for love and companionship. The vast scope of relationship issues is best evident from the ongoing frictions and problems in our own or other families as well as the growing percentage of marriage breakdowns. In all, the level of deficiencies and deprivations caused by love and loneliness in modern societies make the topic of relationships quite sensitive and important for individuals and society as a whole. We are facing a major crisis and nobody seems to know how to go about tackling it, either. In fact, nobody seems to really care about this social pandemic, anyway!

Why Marry?

Our *needs* for sex, love, and compassion are natural motives for getting married. Moreover, our cultures and ethics demand that we engage in some formal ritual to make relationships somewhat binding and dependable. The purpose of these rules is to protect individuals, enhance family values, and strengthen the nucleus of social structure. All along, we have learned to expect a stable relationship (preferably a formal marriage) with someone we have spent a lot of time to find and tame. On top of all these natural and cultural motivations, however, these days partners have grown high expectations from relationships in line with their rising personal needs and dreams. These new needs, especially partners' craving for love and attention, have grown drastically in recent decades, thus making the task of relating in relationships difficult. People are obsessed to find happiness, which they believe comes mainly from love and *ideal* relationships. However, this is a bizarre expectation—to make our partners responsible for bringing us that illusive happiness that we seem incapable of finding on our own. We ignore the simple fact that since nobody can find that elusive happiness, expecting it from one another in our relationships is pure silly.

Accordingly, the relationship environment has also become too complex in line with people's rising pomposity, greed, and unreliability. While they seek love and lasting relationships, their sense of commitment to cultural or general family values have diminished. No new guidelines exist, either, to provide at least the basic principles of relating in relationships to keep partners' Egos manageable. Thus, people get into relationships with crooked motivations and idiotic expectations. While they have become oversensitive and obsessed with finding love, they have little compassion and patience themselves. Under this confusing situation, people settle for a companion for all the wrong reasons without any knowledge of relationship needs or even a true sense of love, yet they naively consider 'love' the main success factor for building their relationships. Accordingly, they also get out of their relationships with equally selfish motivations and hasty decisions in pursuit of better companions and more sexuality. People often seem to get married with their calculating minds and agendas, while misperceiving or ignoring the real purposes of relationships.

Often our motive for marriage is merely a change in our monotonous lives. Sometimes, a partner sees marriage merely a means of financial security. In another case, a person lowers his/her standards of an acceptable spouse since s/he is getting old and perhaps her 'biological clock is ticking' too fast. Thus, we jump into a marriage carelessly, hoping that it would work out fine somehow. Both our instincts and need for compassion due to social pressures make us too needy for a partner. Of course, our needs for belongingness and love raise our urge for marriage as well. In fact, our belongingness and love urges have the strongest mental impact on our lives both positively and negatively. They are supposedly medium range needs of humans, but are emerging, nowadays, quite urgently as deeply psychological attachment needs. Considering the fact that our needs for food and security are rather attainable and automatic in modern societies, love and belonging needs stir our minds and psyches the most all our lives. In that sense, 'search for a companion' manifests as a basic human need, since we crave it so intensely and passionately, and yet often fail to satisfy it properly, if at all.

Overall, it is becoming difficult to assess partners' (often crooked) personal motives for starting a relationship beyond the natural needs of humans (for a companion). Obviously, all these doubts and decisions have incredibly high consequences on our lives' quality, either positively or negatively—mostly negatively, nowadays. Anyway, an assessment of our motives (both our own and partner's motives) is needed before making a decision or committing ourselves to a binding relationship.

Surely, life is more beautiful and tolerable when our choice of a companion turns out positive and we have a peaceful, pleasant life with someone we love, care for, and understand. A compatible and agreeing partner brings the most gratifying experience for a normal person with average intelligence.

Conversely, if our decision turns out bad, which seems to be most likely, nowadays, the repercussions are often extensive and destructive. Decisions about marriage normally result in one of these extremes, although some couples learn to live peacefully together in spite of their conflicts and differences. These facts seem to be obvious and commonsense. Yet, most of us fail in our decisions for many reasons and end up in a marital entrapment or opt for separation. More than half of marriages in North America lead to divorce. Another majority of couples live somewhat separately or desperately in doomed affairs all their lives with no guts to get out of them.

If we believe we are so smart when we are making our marriage decisions, why are most of us failing? The answer is that, we do not know what we are really getting into. More importantly, no longer any reliable norms and guidelines exist for couples to plan and manage their marriages, while their vast Egos and misperceptions keep raising their expectations from relationships. In all, it seems that we are wrong in our decisions because:

i) We are unaware of the real purposes of marriage outside our physical attraction to another person and our selfish, high expectations about martial life.
ii) We do not know enough about relationships' unique needs and the person we are planning to marry.
iii) We are not familiar with the harsh realities of married life beyond our limited observations of our parents and maybe some friends or relatives.
iv) We do not even take our parents' dire marital experiences seriously, because we think we are immune to their types of mistakes and problems.
v) We do not analyse enough our own or partner's motives for getting married, or ignore them for some emotional or practical reasons.

We often let our naive needs, love, and loneliness affect our marriage and divorce decisions prematurely before weighing the risks and demands of relationships properly. Actually, we (especially women) often seem to spend more time, logic, and energy on simpler decisions, such as purchasing a pair of shoes, compared with divorce and marriage decisions, *relative to their long-term risks and impacts on our welfare, of course.* We feel obliged to rather justify our decision to buy those shoes logically (because we have to pay for it), instead of emotionally per se (just because we like it). We endure a grave dilemma weighing the shoe's quality, our need for it, where we are going to wear it to, its price, etc. We try to prove our logic, rather than being emotional.

Yet, considering the lifetime enormous risks of marriage, **couples do not study all the right factors and their motives properly.** We dismiss relevant relationship factors in favour of irrelevant factors listed in Chapters One and Two.

Sadly, we often lose our logic and foresight prematurely when lured by love and sex or the mirage of marriage. We feel too lonely to worry about the sad state of relationships these days. And often we opt for divorce on the big assumption that a more suitable mate is waiting for us out there.

Of course, we take a lot of time supposedly thinking and evaluating our options and decisions. However, our hesitations and doubts about marriage or selecting a companion do not necessarily mean we are studying the matter logically or the right factors, which we are usually not even aware of, anyway. Especially during the courting period, we are overwhelmed by many thoughts and emotions that are more distracting than helpful for a proper assessment. We usually get swayed by our infatuation and sexual needs; we think we must compromise; or we might ignore or undermine our preferences, purposes, and intentions for choosing a companion. We do not give enough weight to the importance of this decision, because we are unaware of the repercussions of bad marriages—a growing epidemic, nowadays. Overall, considering the magnitude of marriage decisions, we have not learned how to define and study the relevant factors of relationships' success. We do not spend nearly enough time to learn and apply proper criteria to gauge marriage variables and situations. Heck, we do not even have any guidelines and criteria to use, anyway.

Therefore, any wise, logical person cannot stop wondering, "Why get married in this hectic environment?"

The answer is obvious, of course! Among all our needs, belongingness and love put the biggest strain on our psyches and we seem unable to stop seeking a companion obsessively. We are just too adventurous, rather intuitively, about the risks we are taking, since finding a right mate has become so urgent and challenging. A trustworthy companion makes the biggest impact on our psyches, as the outcome affects our emotions and life outlook permanently. Companionship provides great happiness when it is successful. However, remember, it causes extreme pain and disappointment when it leads to arguments, failures, and separation. Sadly, the latter case is becoming more prevalent. Marriage is certainly a big change, but it is usually a change for worse, as statistics indicate. Keeping both our companion and ourselves happy in a relationship is just too damn difficult, nowadays.

By the way, humans' long list of obsessions for many things, including shoes, love, or happiness, shows our innate irrationality and rashness about our needs and plans, instead of studying and fulfilling them with patience. Driven merely by our naïve obsessions for love and happiness, financial gains, or mushy emotions, we forget to measure relationships' needs and complexity enough in advance. We are simply too naive about life, as we are hypnotized in a world of illusions.

We (especially women) buy a lot of shoes, after all, despite all our scrutinies! Why? Are we buying all these shoes merely to forget our relationship and loneliness pains?!

Epilogue

Solutions for marital conflicts are rare and relative. Most of us do not even understand the problems, or make our selfish diagnosis quickly. Yet, recognizing the universal relationship problems that inflict most families has now become urgent. We must believe that partners' idiosyncrasies, incongruity of objectives, high expectations from relationships and life, and miscommunications play essential roles in causing alienation, intolerance, and misunderstandings. These hurdles have now become epidemic with similar natures and causations.

Accordingly, we must also doubt the possibility of finding a partner even remotely compatible with us, or able to build a relatively quiet life together. Our personal experience would definitely confirm the statistics about all these facts. Still, we could learn what kinds of personality adjustments, through self-awareness and using Model, are useful and what kinds of sacrifices we should make just for having a companion.

The health of relationships is essential for keeping couples' hardships manageable and making relationships objective and meaningful again. However, it is even more crucial and urgent for maintaining socioeconomic welfare. Especially in modern nations, the deteriorating social condition makes the study of relationships highly urgent and sensitive, as a *basic* personal need, but also a complex socioeconomic crisis.

Marriage conundrums are deep-rooted and they will keep soaring along with partners' rising expectations, impatience, and intolerance. No remedy seems in sight and not enough research is underway to find a solution. The ideal would be to develop a screening process to at least prevent clearly unfit marriages at the outset. Then, we need an effective process to educate partners initially about the specific needs and hassles of relationships in the new era. We also need substantive therapeutic procedures to help tainted marriages. The whole social structure has been damaged by relationship diseases, as witnessed by rising marriage deaths and incurable sicknesses. Meanwhile, individuals continue to suffer and live with this epidemic helplessly. The sad fact is that the situation would only get worse in the 21st century. Governments' immediate attention and commitment to research are needed to change social and individuals' mentalities about the real purposes of relationships and for finding more practical mechanisms to deal with this matter. So far, governments and legal systems have only caused more problems than solving relationship conundrums. They are only dealing with the symptoms of this pandemic, instead of understanding and curing the roots of the problem. We surely need a new approach and mentality about social values that cause such fatal marital diseases.

We must teach practical guidelines for relationships at high schools very seriously. Couples must also spend a few months completing certain educational requirements before rushing into marriage. They should take courses in conflict resolution, teamwork mentality, and negotiating techniques. Surely, these crude measures feel against natural laws, but no longer natural laws drive marital relationships of modern societies. Marriage has turned into a calculating enterprise, thus requires proper contemplation and education. We need lots of good theories and guidelines to bring objectivity back into relationships. For now, we should **'think divorce at the time of marriage,'** and vice versa, as a potent precautionary vaccination.

www.ingramcontent.com/pod-product-compliance
Lightning Source LLC
La Vergne TN
LVHW090936080826
845145LV00003B/776

9781988351063